Cherished

A Mother and Daughter's

Journey to the Cross

Table of Contents

Prologue

Dear sweet reader, I believe that you have this book in your possession for a purpose and that you are drawn to reading it because Jesus has a call on your life. (He has a call on everyone's life to be His Son or Daughter and to fulfill awesome unique purposes that only each one can, according to Ephesians 2:10.) As you turn each page and embark on this adventure with me, I pray that the Holy Spirit will reveal the Lord Jesus to you in a way that captivates your heart for all eternity. If you know and love Him, may you grow in greater fellowship with Him as you turn each page. I pray that you will laugh and cry with us along the way.

Names have been changed across every chapter as each person described on our journey deserves privacy. My story is one I longed to share to be obedient to the Lord and yet simultaneously honor our family. The testimonies shared are true and the miracles of the Lord never cease. He is healing, saving, comforting, and resurrecting lives today. My husband, children and I have seen and heard of hundreds of miracles in the past many years and know we will be witness to many more. Our God's arm is never too short to save!

The sections written in third person are in one distinct font as this perspective allows for better understanding for the reader. The remainder of the book is told in first person by me in the predominant font style in order to distinguish these two writing styles. I hope you enjoy this reading journey despite the literary style changes that I employed in attempts to divulge more details along the way.

Finally, all of the dialogue has been manufactured based on memories, recollections, and conversations with loved ones to piece together events. Direct quotes during miracles involving our children are salient, and I have used as much original language as my memory would provide.

Cedar is a fictitious town representing many blue-collar towns around America. The details of Daisy's childhood are very loosely based around memories my Mom shared over many decades. The remaining details were added from my imagination. Other town names that are used are the actual places where restaurants, hospitals, churches, and homes were actually located. We lived in Illinois for five decades and have a plethora of incredible memories from the places visited amongst these pages. We cherish the people each one of these places and events represents and hope you will delight in "visiting" as well.

Chapter 1:   Cedar (Illinois)

Matthew 19:14 - Jesus said, "Let the little children come to me, and do not hinder them, for the kingdom of heaven belongs to such as these."

Daisy's petite nose pointed skyward as she sniffed the crisp December air catching snowflakes on her pink cheeks. Her innocent silhouette shaded the sidewalk as she waited for her brother and sister to walk to church on this chilly Christmas Eve. She had an insatiable curiosity for the beauty all around her.... "Why is the sky blue? How do the clouds look like puffed up cotton balls? Could it be possible that every snowflake is unique like fingerprints?" Her mind perpetually raced with thoughts uncontainably frantic and enthusiastically flitting topic to topic, thought to thought. Her recently polished patent-leather shoes clicked on the concrete with each skipping step on the frosty sidewalk. Mother and grandmother slowly made their way down the cracked sidewalk to the creaky gate leading to the main street towards downtown Cedar.

The small town boasted one Methodist Church with a modest working-class congregation. Looking at the stain-glassed windows, one would find Biblical stories of Jesus' healing miracles, His birth, death and resurrection. There was hope of infinite proportions within those images if only hearts would embrace the giver of all hope, Jesus.

Arriving at church, Daisy stared up at Him, the Savior, on the cross hanging high up in the rafters aloft the altar and smiled. She drank in the quiet solitude within the darkness. A magnitude of peace was tangible here. A sacred hush filled the sanctuary on this Christmas Eve night. For the last portion of the service, candles were passed to each congregant. The flames were spread almost contagiously from one candle to the next until the darkened room was aglow with soft yellow light illuminated from each white waxed candle gripped eagerly in each fist. At close of the service, her family huddled up and made the short yet very cold walk back to 112 Chatham Street in Cedar, Illinois.

The town was riddled with Depression era poverty mindsets and families brilliantly stretching every penny earned and stored in rusty coffee cans. Coin slots were roughly cut on plastic lids and the sounds of each "clink" could be heard as the pennies were eagerly deposited with each payment for work well done.

Daisy and her brother, John, raced to the newspaper factory after school to snatch the latest news and bring it home to share with glee over candlelit dinners. Sunup meant chores of setting the table, polishing shoes, sewing patches and hems, checking for milk jugs on the porch, and packing school books and slates into satchels by the porch door. They rose early each morning to help Mother and Grandmother with breakfast, chores, and dishes before the brisk ½ mile walk to school.

Daisy simply adored learning! Every subject sparkled to life as the teacher would espouse the most precise mathematical calculations, proper grammar and punctuation, as well as geographical places all around the globe. Her synapses crackled to life each moment as she stepped into the classroom and was eager to learn. She would soak in all she could, chattering about it on the walk home with John. Daisy could not stop telling stories, sharing vivid details, and asking hundreds of questions. John was the cautious older brother, a much more subdued and deep thinker who did not easily tire of Daisy's incessant questions. He was a fabulous listener and sounding board, and would teach her all about what he learned in Math and she would be steps ahead of her classmates. They were already doing division and talking about multiples of 20's and 50's and more! How exciting! John was a genius before his time and read high school level books about electricity, Physics, Engineering and longed to use his hands and mind to build and fix things. As a modest family of 5 plus Grandmother to clothe and feed, any repairs he could make around the home to save on expenses was beneficial. Mother worked long days as a secretary at General Electric and their father was in and out of employment with a local factory. As work ebbed and flowed, he would make ends meet delivering milk in an old stick-shift milk truck with a sliding door. The cost to raise a family of three youngsters with hungry mouths to feed and growing bodies to clothe raised to a lofty $200.00, annually. In middle America in 1952, the cost of wood, coal, and rising demand for bolts of fabric to sew homemade clothing made prices skyrocket. Post World War II economics were challenging, to say the least. Sharing clothing between Daisy and her younger sister, May, and getting hand-me-downs from wealthy city cousins got them through many years. A majority of families in Cedar did not have the luxury of eating beef and lamb and world-class honey smoked hams for Christmas dinner. Daisy's family worked two full-time jobs, John and Daisy worked part-time delivering newspapers and collecting firewood around town, and still they could only afford a small turkey, potatoes and green beans for their Christmas dinner that year. Around the table that night would be Aunt Jane and Uncle Chuck, Grandmother Mable, Mother, Father, Daisy, John and May.

The pot bellied stove full of coal would puff out clouds of heat to warm the table in addition to banter from the week's events. The next morning, they would look forward to a fresh orange and confectioner's sugar cane in their stockings. This would be a delightful treat once per year they anxiously awaited. After rations had been common all across the land during wartime, Mother still had never gone back to lumps of sugar in her coffee or tea and Grandmother could not bear to drink a full cup of tea with the opulent tea leaves which once graced the bottom of her China teacup. Now, slightly yellowed water was all she could allow herself to enjoy as her family piled onto a tattered rug near the living room "stove" to lay and listen to every Saturday night radio program. Saturday nights were special in their household. Work was completed for the week before sundown so they could bathe, enjoy a meal and some rest around the stove listening to the latest episodes over the airwaves.

When Father returned home from war, he was a shadow of the man he had once been. His body would rest in a chair in their home and barely register the presence of his children in the very room in which they mercilessly chattered and played. Mother would call his name for supper and acknowledged only a faraway look on his countenance until his eyes snapped back to present day. He would slowly convince his legs to obey by walking to the kitchen to enjoy a meal with his waiting family. The shells and trenches, barracks and sleepless nights stole the best of what he had before the winter of 1944. He and his brother had been called up to be deployed to Europe. They enthusiastically piled into buses driving to military bases for basic training preparing to enlist thousands into combat as President Eisenhower implored willing and able-bodied young men to fight for Uncle Sam. With a wife and one baby at home, Father delayed and desired to avoid being called up, but nonetheless, he was needed along with 1,000's of others.

Daisy had not known her father any other way, sadly, without even a faint smile on his lips or any kindness in his eyes. Those were distant memories now. This shadow of a man was short, curt, and easily angered. Time once spent at home helping his wife and playing with Baby John were long since in the rearview mirror. The man who now slept in their home lumbered to work and strolled aimlessly home was wounded in more ways than one. His soul was tormented and fractured by the horrors of war, comrades bombed and maimed by enemy fire and his right ankle mercilessly fractured by shrapnel. The telltale limp in his gait was eternally altered as he emerged from the bus depot that warm summer morning as he returned from the military hospital in Virginia. Although gone only 15 short months, just long enough to have aged 40 years in his heart, mind, and soul, he returned home to Mother and his young son. Daisy was born during his tenure with the Army and he missed her birth and many of her "firsts". He never connected with her, emotionally, and didn't feel like her rightful "father". Their relationship never recovered from his absence. Soon after returning home, Mother was pregnant with Little May. Mother believed the birth of this beautiful blue-eyed blond curly haired girl would put joy back into his life and there was a spark that lasted a short time then the ember faded once again. May became the "light of his life" for a time as she needed to be held, fed and rocked to sleep. As soon as she was old enough to run, race, skip play hopscotch and tear off to school with her older siblings, he became less and less useful to her. His reclusive soul was so broken, he was no longer proficient at holding a reliable job which was necessary to provide for their growing family's needs. He was trapped inside a traumatized prison disguised as his own body and there seemed no way of escape.

Nevertheless, Christmas seemed to possess a certain magic that negated the harsh reality of the day and ushered an innocent anticipation of tomorrow in them as the children went to sleep, dreaming of gifts and festivities surrounding Jesus' birth. Waking up on Christmas morning was always a joyful delight racing down the stairs, rubbing greasy fingers down the well-worn wooden banister and grinning with anticipation. John, Daisy, and May squealed with excitement of looking into their stockings and tearing open the comic-printed wrapping paper on their single gift under the rudimentary tree.

Mother had a tradition of bacon and eggs on Christmas morning with their finest China from their grandparents. They used their Christmas bonus to buy Grade A maple syrup poured from a white Milk-glass pitcher that was Grandmother's. The delectable contrast of burnt crisp salty bacon with sugary sweet and smooth drops of maple syrup was simply a luxury. Daisy could scarcely wait for it every December. Hot and steamy biscuits with cool and creamy homemade apple butter rounded out their breakfast delicacies. May was clapping her little chubby hands, excitedly, as she waited for Grandmother to say "Grace " before they could all dive headfirst into the mounds of food on the doily-lace tablecloth.

"Amen!" proclaimed Grandmother. John's slightly longer pre-pubescent arm was the first one to grab a steaming hot sourdough biscuit from the platter. His knife dove for the freshly hand-churned butter on the dish in the middle of the table. "Save some for me!" cried May impatiently.

"Grandmother made enough for two per person, May, just you will see!" countered Daisy, emphatically, as she took three long crispy strips of bacon fried in lard. Smacks of delight were heard as they ferociously chewed the breakfast fare with zeal.

The clattering utensils slowed as bellies filled and Father pushed his chair away from the table. Mother and Grandmother were next as they carefully carried stacks of plates to the warm soapy water-filled sink. Three exuberant youngsters raced to the tree to play with their toys and shouts of laughter as John pretended to be a train engineer.

Those simple days faded into the background as Father's mental illness increased and was moved to an institution. His violent, aggressive and abusive ways had left a great deal of scars and trauma on his family, especially Daisy and John. Even the most jaded of hearts would be repulsed by the details of how he gruffly destroyed the innocence and trust of their youth. These are scars not made of blood cells and skin which heal and diminish over time and scarcely leave a trace. The depth of these wounds are at the soul level which callouses the human heart, steals joy and hope and leaves skepticism, fear and caution in its cruel wake. John, Daisy and May had their childhoods shatter and a once anticipated "happy family" was left in shambles. Father did more harm to his children than anyone can fathom and any God-fearing person ought never give full vent to the horrors they experienced at his own hands.

In the days that followed, Grandmother's stern, practical but steady care kept the family faithfully marching forward but a permanent shadow had been cast on the doorstep of 112 Chatham Street in Cedar that would never lift for many decades.

Chapter 2:   A Very Hard Day

January 19th, 2023- Central Florida- 7 pm EST

Psalm 118:17- "I shall live; not die and declare the words of the Lord."

On a temperate winter midnight in the ICU of a hospital in a sleepy tropical town, the monitors beeped erratically as the night nurse strolled in and out every 10 minutes like clockwork. I looked at the clock for the 22nd time since arriving hours earlier. "Lord Jesus, we need a miracle and it can *only* come from Your Powerful hand. We *curse* death off my Mom in the Precious Name and by the Blood of Jesus. We release the Heavenly Host of healing, ministering and warring angels to flood this hospital room, in the Name of Jesus, Our Savior. We cancel the assignment of hell and death off Daisy Jane Nowacki in the Name of Jesus and we speak LIFE over her in Jesus' Name. We cancel every spell, hex, vex, hoax, curse and incantation spoken against her and declare that she will see the goodness of God in the land of the living! She will live out the book of life you have for her as you know every day she will walk this earth and every hair on her head. You knit her in her mother's womb and she is fearfully and wonderfully made. As her daughter, I take authority over the enemy and I believe she will be healed in Jesus' Name!" I continued contending for my currently frail mother's life hour after hour over the course of the night. The midnight phone call 24 hours before from my stepfather, Ned, alerted me to the shocking revelation that my Mom had a "routine" medical procedure to scope her abdomen and look for abnormalities, leaving her in unexpected organ failure and in the hospital. My mother was an unstoppable, vivacious, and naturally caffeinated woman who was born with fiery red hair and a personality to match. No one could subdue her enthusiasm and zest for life. When her mind and heart were set on something, take a step back, because she would be steamrolling towards her end goal, whether you were with her or not. The woman I saw in this bed with arms tethered by velcro straps to the metal bars is not the woman I knew.

I flashed back to 6 months earlier as she came to visit our small family in a suburban town in Chicagoland. She surprised us only a few days earlier saying that she would come for 3 quick days as Ned hates to fly, and she planned to drop in and see our teenage kids in between their busy work schedules. My son, Marcus, took his Grandma out for drives jamming to 70's tunes she knew growing up and out for coffee. This particular hot summer day, she forgot to order "decaf" from the barista at the bougie riverside coffee shop. Once the orders arrived and cool iced java swam on their lips, she revealed, "Oh no, I forgot to ask for decaf...AGAIN!" Marcus knew this meant the most effervescent version of his grandmother was about to grace the front seat of his hot rod as they sped through the streets on the way back to their home where our family waited for their return. He recounted listening to their favorite songs on high volume, windows rolled down, and shouting the lyrics to "Don't Mess around with Jim", cruising well in excess of the speed limit past horse farms and into the subdivision. Upon their arrival, Daisy burst through the back door of our two-story home belting out unfamiliar words in a caterwauling voice while playing air drums. The rest of us, knowing Daisy's hyper propensity, saw the coffee cup in hand and thought the same things...."Not decaf again?" We knew that the next 3 hours or so would be quite lively! She immediately went to the basement where instruments, pool table and ping pong were awaiting her like a little girl in an arcade with a brand new roll of shiny quarters. She went around the room trying this and that until she settled onto the drumset stool and began banging mercilessly away. The sound from the kitchen was so unmistakable, and clearly not Marcus' musician-like patterns, that I raced to the downstairs landing, phone camera in hand, while recording the cacophony of sounds. As 77-year-old

Daisy came into view, she was covered head-to-toe with a flurry of limbs as she banged, hit, kick-drummed, and pounded on the bass, snare, drums and cymbals. I burst out in laughter at this sight, realizing that if we can bottle this kind of energy, it would make us legitimate millionaires.

Daisy had always been one of a kind, cut from a different cloth, walking to her own beat (no pun intended), sharp, bold, quick witted and always looking to accomplish something. She had set records at her uptight stodgy Japanese corporate office by taking dictation for and performing secretarial duties for not one, not two, not three, but five Japanese bosses fresh off the plane from Tokyo who were no nonsense in every sense of the word. She typed over 100 words per minute with one error, wrote in shorthand, took dictation, talked faster than an auctioneer, and resolved conflicts and obstacles for her bosses like nobody's business. As she climbed the corporate ladder, she did it in style. Daisy always lived on a shoestring budget and did not afford herself any luxuries or non-necessities. Her slender frame was donned with straight skirts, nylons, heels and solid blouses and blazers that she mixed and matched for decades with simple jewelry. She was professional, polished, and spoke well with impeccable English and grammar beyond her small town education. Her family's modest roots would never betray her speech, her work ethic or her posture as she asserted herself to have a drive and perseverance to do everything with excellence.

The woman in this hospital bed does not resemble the Daisy Jane I know, Lord....what happened? I soon found an answer to my question as she began mumbling almost incoherently. "Mom, I'm here, it's Cassie. I came as soon as Ned called me."

"They're trying to kill me, they want to hurt me, you have to get me out of here!"

"Wait, slow down, Mom, no one wants to hurt you, what do you mean?"

"Dr. B, Dr. B....you have to call him. Get my phone, find his message, he can help me, you have to take me there." The frantic look in her eye was nothing I had seen before and had no idea what led up to these bizarre sets of circumstances.

"Mom, I just got here, let me massage your feet, talk to you, and get you what you need to help you. Let me adjust your pillows so you are more comfortable and you can explain everything." She allowed me to plump up the three flat hospital pillows and position them under her back and neck. I began to massage her feet as we had done for each other for over four decades. I looked up to her face, seeing a yellow-cast to her skin and bloating in her usually thin cheeks. I glanced up at the saline bag dripping into her IV and realized the bloating is surely from the fluids they are giving her in this compromised state.

"You have to take me, Cassie, please, don't tell Ned, I need to get out of here."

"Mom, he adores you and is the most amazing and loyal husband I have ever known. He would *never* try to hurt you in any way and he wants only what is best for you. Just rest while I massage you and let you relax and get some sleep. I'll be here with you all night and as long as needed. I'm not going anywhere."

She mumbled more unintelligible frantic fragments of sentences, repeating herself and her voice began drifting to the background as I set to my task at hand. I will pray for healing, for resurrection of her broken body systems, and believe for ultimate miracles. I began to pray for each cell, her bloodstream, her organs, her liver, kidney, pancreas, her heart and brain, and her blood pressure, oxygen levels, sugar balance and more. I interceded off and on for over 4 hours as she was in and out, moaning in pain. I would look at the monitors and see blood pressure of deathly low levels, 90/50 and began to curse death off her body. The Lord would immediately answer by spiking her pressure up closer to 120 over 80. Oxygen levels began to crash into the

80% range and I would pray and cancel death and the advancement of hell off

her body and her oxygen would soar back into the mid 90% range! God was

doing mighty miracles all night long! My faithful tribe of prayer warriors were

on call near their phones as I texted short updates requesting powerful

prayers for miracles for Daisy all night. Only my closest friend and husband,

James, stayed up almost all 10 hours reading and responding to my texts with

instantaneous prayers.

My mindset all night was on healing. James and I had seen hundreds

or more healings in the preceding 10 years in so many different

environments and locations. We saw street healing ministry, at conferences, in

living room Bible studies, Sunday morning church prayer time, during

deliverance sessions and more. We know and experience the Mighty Power of

Our Healer, Jehovah Rapha. I was at war and on the battlefield of my life. I had

seen the supernatural happen so many times and under every possible

circumstance and I knew the Lord sent me to be alone with my Mom to usher

in the very Presence of Almighty God into that hospital room. "For such a time

as this...." the Lord whispered to me. Yes, one of my favorite accounts in God's

Word is the Book of Esther in which a young, courageous virgin girl Esther has the honor and privilege of interceding for the entire nation of Israel and her

exiles in Persia. Facing genocide, she puts her life on the line and boldly

approaches the king to request they be spared. The Bible deems her who is

needed for this high calling, "for such a time as this". Here I stood in my

Esther moment, knowing that my Mom had never confessed the name of Jesus

in my lifetime, knowing her destiny was not to be dancing in the fields of

Grace with her Daddy God after she took her last breath. I had prayed for her

faithfully for 30 years and invited her to church, Bible studies, to my home to

watch Christian films, to women's Christmas events, concerts, the kids'

Christian school performances, Bible speech meet and much more. James and

I wept together for our lost loved ones and desired more than anything to see

them all give their lives to the Lord and experience His true love, joy, peace

and salvation. These might be the best moments I will ever have with no

distractions, no "to do" list to compete with, and a receptive "audience".

Asking for the Lord's divine leading, I asked Him for the right words,

demeanor, heart to love and serve, and for her heart to be tender and

cultivated to say "Yes!" to Jesus now. I began to sing, "Our God is an Awesome

God", and repeated the chorus numerous times. Joining me was Shane and

Shane from my Spotify app as the hospital room became an altar. I prayed, I sang, I wept, I worshiped, and I ushered in the Lord with my heartfelt, unabandoned worship of Him. He swept in as promised in Psalm 62, which declares, "The Lord inhabits the praises of His people."

I felt the warmth of His presence, the strength of His Power and His love sweep through my heart. The weariness I should have felt inside after 20 hours awake was nowhere to be found. Hunger was absent. Thirst and fatigue were distant strangers. The consistent love of the Lord was evident in each provision of energy, strength, clarity of mind and calm. The most remarkable gift all night long was the constant perpetual flowing stream of God's perfect peace. It was unmistakable yet understated. There was literally not a trace of fear all night long. No fear of death, no fear of what happens if my prayers aren't answered now, no fear of what is next. The only tangible presence was just a mother and daughter in the dark recesses of the night, reconnecting, sharing love, asking forgiveness of things long since past, holding hands, tender words spoken, and enjoyable silence of togetherness. Priceless, tender, unforgettable. Only Jesus.

Carol broke the silence as she came in to check Daisy's vitals again for what seemed like the dozenth time since I arrived before the close of visiting hours.

"If you keep your Mom awake anymore, I am going to have to ask you to sleep in the waiting room," Carol chided.

"No one has ever succeeded in getting Daisy Jane to stop talking. Virtually *everyone* has tried, it is just not possible", I quipped back, defending myself. "She has a mind of her own."

"Let her rest as best you can then. May I speak to you in the hall for a moment?"

"Sure." I quietly set Daisy's hand on the bed as she intermittently moaned from pain, incessantly trying to find a comfortable position for her restless body.

As we stepped past the glass doors into the desolate ICU corridor, Carol whispered somberly, "Do you realize that your mother is in active organ failure?" Silently, I prayed, "I break off those words in Jesus' Name!" Aloud I replied to Carol's question, "Can you please explain what has happened since Tuesday? I have no idea how a routine scope can lead to organ failure. Surely there are a bunch of missing puzzle pieces here. None of this makes any sense."

Carol proceeded to show me the transcribed notes from doctors since intake early Tuesday afternoon by the ER attending physicians, to the 2nd floor doctors who saw her for one day until being admitted to the 4th floor ICU on day three. The kidney numbers and stats, blood levels, oxygen, medications administered, notes, heart rate, and details were there ad nauseam. My head was spinning with facts and information, but I asked the Lord to give me understanding beyond my medical knowledge. Terminologies stood out from years of watching medical trauma shows and reading dozens of thriller novels and suddenly, the state my Mom was in began to unfold. Creatinine levels were too high. This meant her kidney was in distress. Daisy had surgery at just 21 years of age to remove her non-functioning kidney that had never developed since birth. Once removed, she was prone to more bladder infections and UTI's and knew her one kidney would have to last her all of life. The night before, I had just assured Ned that if I am a match, I will volunteer a kidney in a heartbeat. He had gone home knowing there is "hope" on a humanistic level that if she is in kidney failure, she can perhaps receive a healthy one from me.

I peppered Carol with medical questions and curiosities of the "what if" they can drain the fluid from her abdomen after first rounds in the morning?

"What if they can give her some food or water despite the diagnosis of pancreatitis?" I asked.

"We have *never* been a medication family and do not look to western medicine to solve any of our problems...my Mom would not ask for help in this way, but clearly she is in agony and cannot sleep for even 4 minutes at a time. Can you give her a topical analgesic? Can I put essential oils on her, something?"

"When the doctor comes for 7 am rounds he can assess your Mom's condition and make a decision then. We have no one to approve any change in care or prescriptions to the pharmacy until then. Pancreatitis requires a typical protocol of 7 days of no food or water, only intravenous fluids," Carol replied, matter-of-factly.

Shock and bewilderment over the broken state of American medicine reeled in my mind. If she cannot sleep, how can her body heal? If she is in this much agony, she cannot sleep. This is a catch 22! We ask you, Lord, Our Healer! You are the One we look to! "Some trust in princes and some trust in chariots, but we trust in the Name of the Lord!" This familiar Psalm flooded my consciousness as I knew another dead end was being broached. "Father God, my Mom is in so much pain and cannot sleep for even a few short minutes. I ask you to lay your hand on her and remove the pain in Jesus' Name."

I rarely left my Mom's side for even 2 minutes to use the bathroom. I do not remember eating, drinking, or going to the bathroom for more than a rapid trip down the hall to call James before 10 pm to provide an update and pray together for my Mom. I massaged lotion into her hands, put lip balm on her chapped lips, and stroked her hair lovingly with my hand. I spoke to her and over her the Truth of the word and sang worship music off and on for hours, quietly.

Through her oxygen mask at one point, I heard some words croaked out and saw fog fill the clear plastic guard. As I edged nearer to her, I pulled the mask down to hear her repeat lines of the song back to me, "Our G-o-d, is an awe—-some G-od."

"Yes, He is !! He is awesome, Mom! YES!" I was so excited to know she is actually acknowledging Him as God and awesome! I continued praying, perpetually, "Wow, Lord, keep softening her heart to you, Lord! This is so amazing and you are infinitely good. You want NONE to perish and all come to repentance (II Peter 3:9), you say in your word, and you did not come to earth to appoint us unto wrath but unto Salvation (I Thess 5:9). Your Word is so clear. You desire for her name to be in the Lamb's Book of Life (Rev 21:27) ."

I continued texting James and my prayer coverage from our Monday night group of 20 plus people, called The Remnant. They are so steadfast to pray night and day, day and night! We are so blessed to have dozens of men and women who simply adore the Lord and desire to be watchmen on the wall for all Creation, and especially for His Bride. They are the most reliable soldiers in this spiritual battle. Every request, every need, there will be a dozen or more responses to prompt and urgent prayer needs on our text thread. I began sharing some of their answers to my Mom's plight throughout the night.

"Mom, Lydia just sent this prayer...oh, now Evangelina, and Noni, they are up praying, Mom! They trust the Lord to heal you. He is Our Healer. We are going to keep asking."

Abraham had taken his long-awaited, one and only begotten son, Isaac, on a multiple day journey up a mountain with firewood knowing he was about to sacrifice him to His One true God, Yahweh. Did Abraham think he was going to lose Isaac? No. Did he think all of this would end in death? No, I do not think so, ultimately. I only share this to say that Abraham's belief was counted to him as righteousness, the Lord tells us in Romans chapter 4, and we see his faith was bold and strong. Did he believe the Lord would resurrect Isaac after the sacrifice? Perhaps. Abraham loved the Lord and he trusted. I connected my faith to Abraham's that night because not for *one* moment that night did I believe my Mom's actual life on earth would ultimately result in death. I had prayed 30 years for her salvation, fasting dozens of days and times at pivotal junctures in her life on which her life seemed to hang in the balance, and I wasn't going to believe for one moment that 30 years of tears and prayers were going unheard for even a nanosecond by Our Perfect Heavenly Father. He never slumbers nor sleeps (Psalm 121) and he will never leave nor forsake me (Heb 13:5). Knowing His word and His character, I knew He has the power to bring beauty out of even the hottest and most destructive of ashes (Isaiah 61). Would her organs die and He would resurrect them? I believed He would. I had seen too many similar miracles to doubt for a blink that He would not. Would He bring her a new kidney to replace the missing one? He can! Would he? I didn't know. Would he remove the pain supernaturally as He had for our son, Marcus, when he broke his foot the night before varsity soccer tryouts for the school's State Championship run? He had done that for numerous people that we knew and read about for years.

Of course he can remove pain. Will He allow her to sleep even when she wants to chatter perpetually after three sleepless nights? Yes, He can, but would He?

This was all a complete mystery to me. I pondered many questions and my faith simply told me to keep laying hands on her broken and pain-riddled body and rebuke death over and over again. And I did. He answered, repeatedly. Sundown, through to midnight, then on to 2 am, He kept answering. Shortly thereafter, I began to worship more fervently with powerful songs that would invite angelic presence into this dark hospital room on the 4th floor on that January day. "Power in the Blood", "Speak the Name of Jesus", and more songs flooded the tiny glass-boxed room in which we had our mini curtained "sanctuary". I stood with my hands held high and proclaimed the Name of Jesus over my family, mental illness, weakness, infirmity, depression, anxiety, cancer, sickness, and disease....and proclaimed the Name of Jesus over DEATH!! I read and agreed with more prayers being texted from one thousand miles away from James, Evangelina (my dearest sister in Christ for over 20 years) and a dozen women from our prayer groups. The Truth in their prayers lined up with Scripture and Heaven. God's presence kept penetrating the darkness. It was time for me to talk about Jesus and really express the Gospel in simple terms for my Mom to humbly agree to and accept.

"Mom, you have been the most self-sufficient woman I have ever known. You have been strong-willed and done things your way. Right now, you cannot even scratch your own chin. Your arms are strapped to the bed because you wanted to make a jailbreak so they tethered you to the guardrails. Times in your life when unspeakable acts were done to you, the Lord wept tears as your heart broke. He has always been with you and never wanted you to be mistreated in all the ways you were. He tells us in His word that He stores every one of your tears in a bottle and He adores you. He wants you to know Him and to love Him, but you have to say yes to Jesus. Jesus loves you, laid His life down for you, and wants you to be with Him forever. You need to say yes to Jesus."

As I sang a worship song, which might have been, "Jesus, loves me, this I know, for the Bible tells me so," she finally replied to my prayers, words and songs with a croak from under her mask..."I lo-o-ve Him with e-v-ery cell of my body."

AWESOME, JESUS! To hear these beautiful words out my Mom's own lips is music to my ears and music to Heaven, I am sure! Is she saved, Lord? Does she know you yet? I don't know what just happened, but I am content to know that she is saying "Our God is an Awesome God and I love Him with every cell of my body." This is so incredible, Daddy. You allowed me to spend these last 5 hours with my sweet Mama, massaging her feet, stroking her hair, holding her hand, making things right, asking forgiveness, apologizing for gaps in our relationship, telling her of my deep love for her, sitting in the quiet and getting to care for her and serve her in a way I never have before. Dare I say this has been one of the best days of my life with her? She never let me help her. She wouldn't sit still long enough to let me serve her. She was always serving others and not just simply receiving. This is a precious gift I never imagined having to experience with my one and only mother, the one who gave me birth. Wow. How could a night of so much suffering and physical pain actually be one of joy in my heart? The dichotomy of joy in the midst of great anguish has a supernatural reality. I was experiencing the Lord and a tender side of my Mom that had never all connected at one simultaneous moment like this in my five decades on earth. Never could I have imagined or orchestrated such a divine experience. But God.

Chapter 3:   Corey and Ned

Ecclesiastes 3:4 - "And a time to heal... a time to build up, a time to weep, and a time to laugh, a time to mourn, and a time to dance."

In the summer of 1983, the weather was mild and humidity high as

Daisy and Cassie moved into their new ground floor apartment. The

complex was utilitarian in design with plain monotone bricks up every side

of the buildings. A grassy courtyard was housed in the interior u-shaped

contour of the complex with three stories of wrought-iron balconies

overlooking it. They toted their meager possessions up and down the

stairway to the half underground garden apartment from their rusty Monte

Carlo parked nearby. Upon walking into their new digs, Daisy proclaimed,

"This is just what I was hoping it would be!" Cassie ran to scope out the

two bedrooms and bathroom down the short corridor just past the cozy

dining room. There would not be much furniture going into this new

dwelling, but two people with love for one another would fill it up quite

nicely. Surveying the space, Daisy made quick work of rearranging her

cookbooks, spices, dishes and glassware. She had a culinary knack that was

known to many to be her specialty. Cooking recipes from all over the globe

is something she pursued with delight and anticipation. One night, homemade egg rolls were on the menu with fresh wonton wrappers, the next Japanese beef "boiled" on a table skillet set at 400 degrees. With Daisy, you never knew what would be served on your plate. It was a welcome treat to sit down to dinner and be "surprised" by her culinary creations.

Cassie, now 7 years old, was a very picky eater, however, and often turned her nose up at whatever meal was put before her. Many evenings, dinner ended with a timer being set and limited minutes in which to clear her entire plate. This was the worst part of the day by far. She would stare and stare and stare at the liver and onions or broccoli heads which were so incredibly bitter. "Who actually *likes* these disgusting things," she thought in utter anguish as the minutes dragged by. There would not be spankings or threats, just Mom's somber tone of disappointment if Cassie didn't obey her. That was the worst….no punishment could even come close to Daisy looking intently into her daughter's deep brown eyes and saying, "I am disappointed in you, Sweetheart." Those were like daggers to her heart! The broccoli, brussel sprouts, or liver and onions would have to be mercilessly chewed and swallowed before she could get up from the table and run and play. Open wide, down the hatch, and onto a night of freedom. At last.

Those days were full of youthful innocence, playing in the courtyard with neighbors, kicking the soccer ball, playing catch, throwing frisbees, and hide and go seek until the sun went down. As school approached, the long days running and playing in the hot sun would be replaced with long bus rides to and from third grade, days of learning and studying and recess in the yard. Cassie absolutely adored everything about school just like her mother. She could not wait to meet her new teacher, Mrs. Knudsen, and classmates who incessantly chatted with her all day long in and out of class. Whispers when Mrs. Knudsen was busy in the room filled the 2nd row where Cassie sat. She was a precocious and lively child who never sat still unless immersed in a novel. Her two closest friends, Sara and Shelly were in her homeroom and they played "chase" with the boys at recess. Those were light and frivolous days with seemingly no cares and the reality of their meager financial means never troubled her for a moment.

Daisy worked two jobs in order to provide for herself and young daughter. She was an executive secretary by day and Mary Kay cosmetics consultant by night. There were evenings she would be gone all day typing and taking dictation, rush home for a rushed dinner with Cassie, then out the door to host a "show". Selling makeup in the evenings allowed Daisy to buy a bed, dresser, and black and white TV for them for only $75.00 from a widower in need of downsizing after his wife suddenly passed. Finally, Cassie had a real bed for herself! Wow, how amazing it was to feel like a princess! The dining room table, covered in fuzz from the felt tablecloth donning it for decades prior, would have to be painstakingly rubbed off with cotton and nail polish remover. The smell of the solvent lingered for days in their tiny apartment. Finally, the wood veneer was smooth and visible. Daisy spruced up the table with fresh placemats and a decorative napkin holder.

Finally, the two girls would eat their meals outside the tiny breakfast nook and in the alcove of the dining room. They could now cook in the kitchen and carry plates and bowls around the corner, through the doorway and set two placements and place settings on the table. It felt formal, it felt special, it felt....right. This cozy apartment was beginning to feel like home. There was room for two more at the table, and additional space when using the optional thick wooden leaf to the center, but for now, two would suffice.

One afternoon, Cassie hopped off the school bus and went racing to her back door. She was careful not to disclose to many that she was a "latchkey" kid in those days. She wore a metal-beaded chain around her neck with a sole, silver key that let her into both the backdoor and her apartment door. Bounding up the three cement steps to the heavy brown metal door, she glanced around and quickly pulled the key up and out, unlocked the door, and rushed down the flight of six steps to the garden apartment door. There, Cassie made sure she was alone, hearing no stairs from the flights above, unlocked their apartment door and slipped inside. She immediately went to the record player and cranked up Michael Jackson's "Thriller" as she danced around on the living room rug. Dancing and singing to her favorite artist was one of her beloved pastimes. Donning an invisible white sequined glove and moonwalking backwards on the carpet, lifting her right leg up to her knee in the air and doing her best MJ impression, Cassie belted out "Beat It". When the song ended, she changed into her Snoopy terry-clothed tank top and shorts and ran outside to see what sports she could play before Daisy drove into the parking lot shortly after 5:00 pm.

Upon scurrying up the flight of stairs and down the concrete steps, she saw two new people she had never seen in their courtyard. A man and boy were playing catch with old leather Wilson baseball gloves, worn and loved over years of use. They talked and ran around as they threw and sometimes missed their targets. Cassie observed them for several moments before boldly walking up to the boy, "Can I play with you?" He looked down at his glove and then to his father and said, "Sure, why not?"

"I don't have a glove", Cassie replied.

"You don't need one", he answered.

"Okay!" Cassie agreed. The three of them began throwing and tossing the baseball around, she lost track of time and realized she needed to ask them their names before departing for dinner. "Sorry, my name is Cassandra. Most people call me, Cassie. What's your name?" she asked the boy.

"Corey", said Corey. "This is my Dad, Ned."

"Hi, Ned! That's a cool name. That is my favorite male name from Nancy Drew! I've read all of her books so far."

Ned chuckled, "I hear that a lot. Nice to meet you Cassie."

Just then, Daisy's silver Monte Carlo rolled slowly into a yellow-striped parking place just off the courtyard. "Well, I gotta go. Great to meet you! Thanks for letting me play!" And just like that, the little girl sped to hug her Mom and head in to make dinner.

Many more after school play sessions ensued as the shadows grew longer and evenings grew shorter as summer drew to a close. Ned, Corey and Cassie played frisbee, catch, kicked soccer balls, and they talked about school, life and the weather. Occasionally, squirrels would join them and the neighbor girls, Tara, and Meredith would run down from their third-story apartment and tag along.

One evening, Daisy's silver car pulled in again at the predictable time about quarter after five, and Cassie said her hasty "good-byes" and ran to hug her Mom. As Daisy emerged from the car carrying her work bag, she warmly greeted Cassie and asked about her day. For the first time, Ned and Corey wandered over to meet her after weeks of time getting to know Cassie, of course they long since should have met her mother, but the occasion had rarely presented itself. Ned slowly approached this gorgeous woman, dressed in her formal work attire, as he looked down at his denim jeans and worn-out gym shoes. He extended his hand towards her saying,

"Hi, my name is Corey and this is my son, Ned." Blood soared through his cheeks as embarrassment raced heat up his torso, neck and into his face. How could he have made such a foolish mistake, and with such a beautiful woman!

Recovering from his blunder, he corrected himself, "I mean, I am Ned and my son's name is Corey. We've spent a lot of time with Cassie and thought it was due time we introduced ourselves." Pausing for courage and wondering what she must be thinking of him at this point, he plunged ahead, "Can I take you out to pizza?"

Daisy falsely assumed he meant just to have Cassie tag along with the boys as they grabbed a bite to eat in town, but she was quickly set straight. "Oh, I guess Cassie could go to dinner, but I already had chicken thawing all day."

"No, I mean," he stammered, "Can I take you, can we take you, both out for pizza? Tonight?"

Daisy was the one now to return the blush as she realized perhaps Ned had been gathering up the courage to ask her out for a while now, yet she had never even spoken to this man.

"I suppose. Yes. Yes, we will need time to freshen up. Um, say about 15 minutes or so?"

"Sure. Yes, okay, 15 minutes will be perfect, right Corey?"

Corey nodded in agreement. " We guys can be ready in a flash. Okay, we will see you out here at about 5:30 and I'll show you to our car," Ned offered.

Just like clockwork, Ned and Corey were dressed in cleaner clothes, ready to drive into town for an adventure they would not soon forget. Ned had on his red and white pin-striped short-sleeved shirt and clean blue denim, with bright white gym shoes. Corey was always found wearing thin cotton t-shirts and loose fitting shorts to match. His white elastic socks far up his shins were inside a pair of blue scuffed running shoes.

The boys walked to Daisy's back entry door and knocked. The girls quickly emerged and they all four walked to the maroon Cougar waiting in the parking lot just as Ned had promised. He opened the passenger door for the ladies as Cassie scurried into the spacious backseat with her buddy. Daisy pulled her long thin high-heeled feet gracefully into the car and before she could reach for the door handle, Ned was already closing it for her in a chivalrous way. Daisy smiled and nodded at his impeccable manners.

Ned drove the four of them cautiously down the streets, past familiar strip malls, and to the local Pizza Hut. They walked in and the hostess asked, "How many?" Ned proudly replied, "Table for four." He was beaming yet nervous with a gorgeous single lady like Daisy near him and two chattering children nearby.

"Dad, can we have quarters? They have Pac-Man and Frogger!"

Cassie sat back cautiously waiting for Ned's response, not wanting to be too eager to ask for money from him. Her mom was super frugal, never wasting a dime on anything, even using nail polish to repair runs in her nylons, so never had she been afforded the luxury of stand-up arcade games like this in public.

"Sure….I'll give you 4 each…don't spend it all in one place!" he answered, chuckling. The kids raced to the corner of the waiting room with their shiny quarters and chose a 2-player game of Pac-Man to start. Always extremely competitive, Cassie planned to knock Corey's block off in every game they played that night. The kids, now occupied while they waited for a table, gave the adults a chance to begin talking. Daisy sat there taking in the sights and smells of the pizza restaurant and had an indelible "deja vu" moment that she spoke of until she was well into her 70's. As they walked in, gave their name for the waiting list, observed the red vinyl booths and juke box along the front wall, the video games and bustling salad bar, she felt like they had been there a hundred times before. She had never seen Ned before and had never been to this eating establishment before, but it felt like they were already a family and this was "their place". Eerie yet overwhelmingly comforting in the moment, the two followed the hostess to their corner booth and began to peruse the menus.

A few moments later, Cassie and Corey came over exclaiming, "She cheated, I would have totally won!" "You would not, I would've beat you anyway!" they bantered. Returning to the table, the kids' arguing overshadowed their parents' requests for which toppings they wanted and finally agreed to buy a large pan crust pizza with half and half toppings to satisfy them all. Cassie, forever the pickiest eater of anyone she knew, would simply pick off the toppings and have the cheese she adored.

The jukebox kept shifting songs between oldies and contemporary hits they sang along to on the top 40 countdowns each weekend. Soon, Billy Joel's "Uptown Girl" made its way over the din of the crowd and the kids began singing, "'Oh oh oh oh oh oh oh, oh oh oh oh oh ohhhh…Uptown Girl, she's been livin' in her white bread world'."

The evening was fun with casual conversation to get to know one another, the kids being, well just kids and making new memories. Daisy and Ned told stories and asked questions of one another. All of the serious conversation of extraordinarily painful and unusual childhoods would wait for another day. Right now, it was just Pizza Hut, the family restaurant where they just might eat 99 times again all together in the future.

Chapter 4:   Daisy in Peril

January 20th, 2023 - 12:00 am EST

John 14:13-14- "And I will do whatever you ask in My name, so that the Father may be glorified in the Son. If you ask anything in My name, I will do it."

Carol the night nurse came in on her continuous 10-minute intervals and beckoned over to me again. "Can I talk to you for a moment?" She gestured to follow her into the desolate and dark ICU hallway where only one nurse was left in these wee hours of the morning at the desk. Not a creature was stirring, not even a mouse. The fluorescent lights hummed on the ceiling, monitors beeping from a half-dozen rooms up and down the l-shaped corridor, and keys tapped on the keyboard as the charge nurse inputted chart records.

"I want to bring you up to speed on your mother's condition. Do you see these levels indicated by these numbers on her chart? Your mom's kidneys are in failure. I am so sorry to have to say this so bluntly, but your mother is actively dying," she said casually.

Again, I muttered under my breath, "I break off those words in Jesus' Name!" I knew to never agree with a bad health report and believe what the Lord says about the situation.

"My Mom only has one kidney," I corrected her. She has only had one since she was 21 years old when she had surgery to remove her non-functioning kidney since it was never viable. She has known for 50 years that I would donate mine to her if I am a match."

"That won't be possible in her condition. She needs surgery and dialysis as soon as possible. Your mom has a DNR and she has refused dialysis. I am afraid without other intervention, the doctors may not be able to do anything to stop the organ failure that is spreading throughout her body."

"What do you mean? She has been the healthiest, most vibrant and youthful woman her age that anyone has ever known. She plays pickleball, golf, gardens three hours each day, goes dancing with my Dad and she is never even tired. She has always been incredibly fit, and just a few months ago, was drumming like mad on my son's drum set. This is *not* the woman I know, and I have been praying all night that she will be miraculously healed by the Lord and back to that lifestyle in the near future."

"As of now, the doctor will come on 7 am rounds and will contemplate your mother's condition at that time, but the prescribed procedure to drain her abdomen is too risky in her state. She has pancreatitis and cannot eat or drink for days. She is getting saline and fluid, but she cannot even have ice chips or anything that can aggravate the pancreas."

"Carol, I know we spoke a few hours ago, but my Mom has been moaning every few minutes for the entire night since I arrived. She has never complained about pain in her life and even bailed water once for 4 plus hours until her spine was curved like a shepherd's hook. She is not a quitter, and she does *not* complain. She has *never* wanted to use medicines or drugs her entire life, but she is in agony. Can't you give her something to minimize this pain?"

"She had dilaudid for 24 hours or so, but with the pancreatitis and kidney failure, we cannot risk the toxins overtaxing her organs as they try to detox the medications. Her body cannot process them right now. She is just too weak. I am so sorry."

All I could think was how all of the holistic options I have in my arsenal are 1,000 miles away in Chicago. Essential oils, arnica, rubs, and so many other options that would topically relieve some pain and also go to work on reducing the inflammation. Doctors never understand what patients really need to heal and get over their problems...they are constantly drugging them up and standing back hoping it seems to help the symptoms. What a bunch of poisons are used in these hospitals in the name of the "Hippocratic Oath". Hippocrates would never allow for such abuse! So, I was going to continue asking Jehovah Rapha, Our Healer, for all healing for every organ. I would reach out to the prayer team again and again all night and get them to keep petitioning Our Great God for what *only* He can do.

"Carol, there are some massively huge pieces to this puzzle that I need to wrap my mind around. My Mom was golfing on Sunday, playing games with friends, then went in for a simplistic scope 2 ½ days ago. And now you tell me her kidney is in jeopardy and her pancreas is completely inflamed. How can this possibly have happened? I don't have any idea why a perfectly active and healthy woman goes in for this test and two days later is in ICU and told her organs are ceasing! Please explain these missing pieces to me. I have a decent level of medical knowledge, so just give it to me straight."

"The scope can aggravate the lining of the organs as it goes down to take pictures on the camera. There are risks associated with accidentally scraping the walls as it turns and gathers information for the doctors to see what might be in there. What were they looking for?"

"That's just it, I have no idea! All I know are some peripheral symptoms she has had for months that were annoying her and they wanted to determine what was the cause. Why on earth they would prescribe a dangerous scope for physical symptoms like eczema, rashes, and a cough, I have no idea." Oh, how I wish Ned had told me about these tests they scheduled weeks ago that I knew nothing about, I reflected.

Again, Carole allowed me to scan all inputted doctor's notes from Tuesday at ER intake, through the room transfer on Wednesday, to the ICU transfer up two more floors. Words like "creatinine", "uric acid", "dialysis", and many other terms were very familiar from the 15 years of watching "E.R." with my husband. I knew this creatinine indicator would say whether or not her kidneys could tolerate any more toxins, chemicals, or inhibitors to normal functioning. Knowing she had been on some long-term MAOI's (antidepressants and anti-anxieties) for a decade or more was not giving me a warm feeling at that moment. I wish I could go back and ask my Mom more fervently to agree to healing prayer and letting our friends lay hands on her. I was feeling regret for all those pharmaceuticals she was being poisoned with over an extremely long duration of time. Why hadn't her psychologist and psychiatrist taken her one kidney into account throughout all of these years?

Did they even know she only had one functioning kidney for the past seven decades? "The state of Western medicine is an absolute trainwreck," I concluded mentally. Are people being told to take this stuff for improving their mental health without taking their total physical health into account? Do any of these practitioners talk to each other, consult the MD's and read one another's notes? The compounding and synergistic effects of these chemicals are awful.

I began to fervently pray silently and then loudly as soon as I was alone, "Lord, we need a miracle, and only You can provide it. My Mom needs a new kidney and a new pancreas. I ask you to send Your angelic host to bring her all of the gifts from Heaven that you have at your disposal. You have everything you need to heal her. I am asking you to come and resurrect every broken and dead part of her body, in Jesus' Name and by the Blood of Jesus. Praise you Lord, thank you, Lord, you are a good, good Daddy, we love and worship you, Father. We thank you for Your Goodness and Your Grace! You are such an awesome God. You know what she needs, Lord! Amen."

I stepped back into the shadowy room as monitors and the oxygen mask reminded me of the harsh reality we were facing. There was a profound absence of fear. An even more marked absence of fatigue and hunger. The

Lord was upholding me by His Righteous Right hand, and it was extraordinarily evident in every area. I ate around noon in the airport and now it just ticked past 1:30 am and food, water, and sleep were nowhere to be found. I was on a mission of the greatest battle for my Mom's soul, and I am not going to sleep on the job. Lord, what next?

Turning on another praise song on my Spotify app, I paced through the tiny glass-enclosed room partitioned by the curtain. This is our sanctuary, Mom. Worship time, just you and me! "I Speak Jesus" came onto the playlist and I paced through the room, inviting angelic host to flood the room with the Father's Presence from Heaven and proclaimed and declared that she was healed, sealed, delivered and whole! The Greek word, sozo, denotes those four traits that can scarcely be nuanced in English and is an incredibly powerful word used in the New Testament. I quoted verses that popcorned into my mind, "I declare my Mom will live and not die (Psalm 118), and see the Goodness of God in the land of the living (Psalm 27). Your word says that you command your angels concerning us to guard us in all our ways, they will bear us up on their hands, lest we strike our foot against a stone (Psalm 91:11-12). You say in II Peter 3:9, you want *none* to perish and all to come to repentance! Lord, that means you want my Mom's name in the Lamb's Book of Life before her last breath!"

Song after song, prayer after prayer, petition after petition, I bombarded the bowls in heaven with incense of my prayers for my sweet Mama. There were going to be no regrets to what I prayed, said or did all night long. My Mom was sleeping about 3-5 minutes at a stretch at most between agonizing groans indicating the pain and swelling in her abdomen were keeping her from rest, incessantly. In these moments, I had a smidgen of time to frantically type out a text to James and my devoted prayer sister, Evangelina. They stayed up 7-10 extra hours awaiting updates, joining me in prayer, and filling those halls with the Lord's presence. My prayer team of sisters in Chicago sent encouragement for many hours. I continued to share these messages to boost my Mom's faith and let her know people are battling on her side and they are standing in the gap!

James was waking up when messages "dinged" on his nightstand and getting cat naps in between with fragments of an hour's sleep here and there. Oh, what a faithful and loyal husband. Even in the massive valley years we walked through in our marriage and the extremely brief mountaintop ones, he was always the most dependable, predictable, and faithful husband and father.

As I watched the monitors monotonously reminding me of the erratic heart rate my mom had at the moment, I allowed myself to meditate on his face and suddenly, his rich blue eyes came dimly into view.

Chapter 5:   The Hot Blond Guy

May 1st, 1996 - Chessie's - Palatine, IL.

Luke 16:13- "No one can serve two masters, either you will hate the one and love the other, or you will be devoted to the one and despise the other. You cannot serve both God and money (or people)."

"What are you gonna do after the store closes tonight?" Mark asked.

"Oh, well, you know, I am home for a week from college, so I don't really have any plans, but I should probably just head home and get some sleep since I'm opening again tomorrow." We were counting our cash drawers at Menards on a cool Wednesday evening in May. I had finished up finals a week early since all the crazy college students at my school attended pub crawl week. This was a week in which a bunch of immature adults frittered away their nights getting blasted before taking the most important exams of the semester and "celebrated" by getting drunk walking from bar to bar. No, thank you! I hated alcohol and the thought of acting like a complete moron repulsed me even more. Going home for an additional eight days prior to graduation, working a chunk off my college loan balance and hanging out with my best friend, Belle, and my parents sounded like a superior plan to me. Besides, I wouldn't be there to see my classmates act like fools and that was another plus. Going home would be a wise decision. What could be better?

"Just come with us!" he persisted.

Snapping back to my cash register drawer, I considered, "Well, I don't like drinking and I don't want to spend money, but I guess I can just go and watch the Bulls 3-peat. That has been the absolute best part of finishing classes early, watching MJ take it to the Miami Heat."

"Sure, whatever floats your boat, Cass," Mark chided.

"Okay, I'll ring out my cash drawer, run to the bathroom, and I will meet you in the parking lot," I agreed, suddenly enthusiastic about the idea.

"Sounds great! Me and Joe from Wallcoverings are walking over together. There will probably be others there who clocked out already."

I walked next door to the bar with my co-workers and met my best friend since high school, Belle, who had driven over from her house in the next town over. She was dressed up, make-up and hair done up to a "tee", her one dimple made her a real eye-catcher for the guys, and her tall frame and heeled cowboy boots were an extra added flair. Her personality was either attractive because of her stubborn sass and crude mouth or it turned guys off in a hot second. Belle had that effect on people. I was the pollyanna girl next door who got called "virtuous" by everyone. I didn't really date until I was 16 or 17 and barely kissed a guy and had avoided spin the bottle and the crazy stuff of childhood that would have rather made me vomit. I wanted a husband, to marry young, have kids, the white picket fence, knight in shining armor, the golden retriever and the American Dream. I wasn't just hoping for it, I counted on it. I had worked too hard for too long to settle for some boring deadbeat existence in some sleepy town with no one whose names were ever put on the map. I was Cassandra Nicole Mueller and I was going to make a name for myself, come hell or high water. I had sacrificed, fought, scraped, studied, graduated 8th in my high school class of 400+ students and on Sunday May 5th, in just 4 days, I was graduating Summa Cum Laude with a perfect GPA at a well-revered Midwest "ivy league" school. No one and nothing was going to get in my way of a successful future, I vowed.

The Menards guys wandered into the back room to shoot pool while Belle grabbed two stools in front of the dart boards and ordered two Madras drinks. It was $1 dollar drink night which brought in the crowds. "Relax, they have pineapple juice and grenadine, it's like a Shirley Temple, don't freak out," Belle scolded me.

"I'm not freaking out, you know how I don't like to drink. Ned's dad was an alcoholic and beat him for years, and the last thing I need is to introduce anything that could remotely be addictive into my life. I'm not doin' it. Period!" I exclaimed.

"Alright, take a few sips and if you don't like it, I'll kill it for you. Deal?"

"Deal." She was so pushy. Why was she my best friend again? Oh yeah, because all four years at college, all I did was study my brains out hoping for a 4.0 and I had zero social life. That's why. Belle stayed home, graduated at 17 and went straight to work at O'Hare airport, saved thousands of dollars, bought her own black Jeep Wrangler in cash at 18, and had a ton of independence while living with her Catholic parents near our high school. Four years later, we had virtually nothing in common, except that we vowed to be virgins until marriage, saved a lot of money so we didn't have to rely on our parents or a husband to take care of us, and we both went to church on Sundays. Other than that, the divergence in our lives had taken a sharp turn since I moved into "ivy league-ville". She constantly called me a "yuppy" even though I had never drank coffee, didn't own my own car, had holes in my old and outdated shoes, and had not a lick of fashion to my name.

"Cassie! Are you even listening to me? Where are you, girl, sheesh!"

"Sorry, it has been a really exhausting week taking finals and working. I guess I spaced out."

"Grab the metal tips and go cash in quarters," she bossed.

"Okay, settle down, are you in a hurry or something?" I queried.

"Yeah, let's play some rounds so we don't miss all of the Bulls' game, alright?" she retorted in her sassy Belle way.

"Yeah, but you can't do both well, you're either gonna let me beat you again, or we are going to see MJ kick some major NBA butt. Which is it?"

Handing her 4 quarters, she said, "Throw to see who goes first. First bullseye wins or best out of three."

I picked up the set of 17mg darts with green flights. Green has always been my absolute favorite color since I was born, I think. I threw left of center, then she hit a Bull, I hit one, and then she hit a second after I missed right. I am the worst at Bullseyes. How can I actually play Cricket every weekend when I am home with her, close all sorts of rounds and somehow miss almost every Bullseye I have ever attempted in my life? It's pathetic.

Just as I was beating myself up for the one millionth time in my life, in walked two preppy college co-ed looking GQ guys. The brunette looked clean cut like he worked at the Merc on the trading floor or as a pedigreed accountant, and the blond dude had a denim hat on backwards and a killer smile. Oh my. I hadn't looked at a guy in months. I was head down, 4.0 GPA, studying 40-50 hours a week, cashiering 3 days a week at Menards, and no fun to my name. Not a lick.

"Did you just see those two guys who walked in?"

"What guys?" Belle asked, cluelessly.

"Don't STARE! 3 o'clock, near the door and walking this way. The blond guy is actually really cute!"

"They are walking over here....hang on."

"Oh no, I am not even remotely ready for this. We came to watch the Bulls!" I said, grabbing her arm.

"Just relax. You never have any fun," she reasoned.

True, I thought. Except when I'm with Belle, and then she lives on the edge and she is hilarious. I would never even dream to do the things she talks about doing and then actually does them! I might be getting in over my head.

"Hi, I'm Ryan," said the brunette. "Ryan, good name," I replied smiling, shaking his hand. The blonde "hot guy" went to get quarters for the dart board. "I'm Cassandra, and this is my friend, Belle." She said something rude I will not repeat, and then up walked "the guy". I think my cheeks flushed pink and embarrassment blazed up my ears as he came to introduce himself. "Hello, I'm James."

"James? Oh no. I told myself I can never date another guy named James for the rest of my life. Long story."

Thinking very quickly on his feet, James quipped, "My fraternity brothers call me Gunnar." "Gunnar," I said, "Good name." Patting the stool next to me, "Have a seat!"

"We saw you girls playing Cricket, mind if we play a game?" James coyed.

Now, I blushed again knowing that for the first time since a super painful breakup that ended an engagement following three years of dating, I was looking at the first guy I actually felt shy around and found incredibly attractive. "Don't blow this, Cassie!" I counseled myself.

"Sure, my name is Cassandra. My friends call me Cassie. We usually play Cricket, but if you prefer 301 we can play. Up to you."

"Cricket is my game...guys versus girls?"

"You're on." James was really good at darts. I knew we didn't really stand a chance. Belle and James were by far the two strongest players, and Ryan and I were surely in their shadows and less confident, but it was a fun game, nonetheless. James and I began talking and getting to know each other a little in between throws.

"Ryan's getting married to the love of his life in 6 weeks and we are out to celebrate the end of bachelorhood," James informed us.

"Really, who is the lucky girl?" I inquired.

"Elizabeth, she's incredible. I bet you would like her," Ryan replied, confidently and beaming.

"Congratulations, that is amazing. What is the date?"

"June 22nd in downtown Oak Brook at the Drake Hotel. We have been preparing for years and saving up since college. I'm gonna marry the girl of my dreams! James just hopes he can find a sweet girl like that someday, too. I tried to tell him, however, finding her will never happen in a bar," Ryan concluded.

My cheeks lit up like fireballs and I wanted to crawl under the table. "I don't like to drink, I didn't party in college, and I have been studying like crazy just to graduate with a 4.0 so I can get a great job, pay off all my debt in 6 months, and move out! I am not like that! I'm not going to let anybody hold me back from being successful," I countered.

Now it was Ryan's turn to look bashful and apologetic. He assumed I was just a "bar girl", which I absolutely was NOT in any respect. I resented being thought of that way and I wasn't going to let him leave thinking I was some cheap hussy and had no morals. That could not have been further from the truth.

"Sorry, I didn't mean you. I mean...I mean, most girls who hang out here are not someone I want to see James settle down with, you know? He's my best friend and it's my job to watch his back."

"I get it, you're a good friend. I'm only home from college for 6 days earning money to save up to pay off my $12,000 college loan and be debt free as soon as I can. I graduate on Sunday. We're just here to watch the Bulls win again tonight. She dragged me out since I haven't been home since Spring Break," I gave a glaring-eyed look at Belle for getting me into this mess. Oh, brother.

As the night went on, we played, chatted, told childhood stories from years past as Ryan snuck out without me seeing him say good-bye and Belle found friends she knew from the airlines. James and I talked from 11 pm until about 2 am when the bar was closing. We all had to be at work before 8 am, including Ryan, whose job was paying for their wedding, so he ducked out to get some decent sleep after his long 45-minute drive back down to the South suburbs. Belle kept checking on me, and we were still talking. She didn't seem mad, so I just kept sharing and asking questions like time was infinite.

We talked about the farm he grew up on, his Mom, church, music, school, his job, where he lived, what car he drove, his vanity license plate, and a lot more. I lost track of the hours and we had the time of our lives. Last call came, and we realized no one would be getting much more than 3-4 hours of sleep, and since my parents lived 40 minutes away in another town, and I worked next door to the bar, I should sleep at Belle's house, which was a quick 15-minute drive. I said good night to James and noticed again how handsome his rich blue eyes were, dimpled smile, gorgeous thick blond locks against his red t-shirt and faded rolled denim shorts.

"Can you drive me home?" James asked brazenly.

"What are you nuts? I don't want my parents reading about me in the paper in the morning, no way! I am sorry, you seem great, but I cannot do that. You could be some serial killer," I paused, "Why, where do you live?"

"One mile down the road, it's about 40 degrees and Ryan picked me up so I don't have a ride. No big deal, I just thought I'd ask. I understand." He grabbed his wallet and keys and made a quick dash for the door after handing me his business card and writing his home phone number on the back. "Just in case. Thank you, it was a great night. I had a blast."

"Me, too. Good night."

Belle gave me a gag me look as she faked putting her finger down her throat and tilted her pony-tailed blond head towards the door of the bar. "Let's go!"

James hurriedly ran the mile home since he was dressed for May daytime temps in shorts and short sleeves, not for these cool evenings that plummeted 30 degrees once the sun went down.

She and I ran to the car in the cool of the night and drove home in a daze as I had stars in my eyes. We talked, I asked her ridiculously cheesy and romantic questions, and she kept giving me cold water answers. I crashed in my clothes next to her after setting her red-light analog alarm clock next to me and curling up in my shirt and jeans under the covers of her double bed. "Do you think he is the real deal?"

"What do you mean, you met him in a bar, he is probably a player."

"But he talked about church, his Mom, and growing up on a farm!" I protested, making my point, or so I thought.

"Cassandra Nicole, you met him in a bar, he probably already has a girlfriend, and he is just playing you. Forget it, forget him, now go to sleep. It's after 3 am and we have to be up at 7."

"Yeah, you might be right, but...". I fell asleep talking about the gorgeous blond guy, James, who brought me out of the nerdy college girl mode and made me feel so "alive".

Chapter 6:   Time to Worship

Jan 20th, 2023 12:30- 2:00 am EST

Psalm 139:14 - "I praise you for I am fearfully and wonderfully made; your works are wonderful, I know that full well."

The monitors shocked me out of my daydream of my husband, James, sitting 1000 miles away awaiting another text from me to tell him best how to pray for my Mom.

"The nurse spoke death over her and I'm REBUKING it, in Jesus' Name. Keep PRAYING!" I texted, brusquely.

"Praying Sweetheart. I'm here. I love you," he texted back with a heart emoji. I am blessed by James, Lord. Thank you for him.

My Mom was mumbling under her oxygen mask again with inaudible sounds, so I drew closer, peeled back the mask an inch or so, and listened intently to what she was saying. "O-ur G-od is…. an Awe-some G-od." I could make out slight staccato sounds sporadically over the extremely loud oxygen blasting into her nasal cavities. This dumb machine was drowning out my Mom's voice and I cannot hear a word she is saying! Can you please let me hear what she is saying? Lord, there has to be something I can make out?

"Cas-sie, I....always loved you...I...love you forever" her faltering voice trailed off.

"Mom, I know! I am so sorry! There were so many things I did and said to you that were harsh and mean, and I was a terrible daughter so many times. I hurt you so badly. I hurt you, and I am so sorry. Will you please forgive me?"

She nodded her matted graying head slightly up and down indicating that she is willing to forgive me. "Mom, I forgive you, too. I forgave you a long time ago!"

Shifting her three pillows and plumping them to better support her aching body, I moved one under the small of her back, one between her folded knees, and the third under her head. "Now, the most important thing you need is rest. We have had an amazing time talking, but the nurse is shooting me the stink eye again, and she is gonna kick me *out* of here, Mom, if you don't stop talking and get some rest!"

I was much more forceful with her than usual, throwing in some humor, hoping Daisy Jane, the most stubborn woman I have ever known, would relent and succumb to true sleep. If nothing else, a restorative nap would help immensely before the 7 am doctor rounds. I still prayed for good news and the uncovering of a miracle the Lord had done while she slept.

Chapter 7: The Courtship

Song of Songs 6:3 - "I am my beloved's and my beloved is mine."

Miracles became common in our family over the years, although when the Lord revealed Himself to us is when we recognized them as such. We probably did not deem them miracles and we most likely glorified "mother nature", "power of positive thinking" or other false gods over the decades instead of giving credit where credit was due. I had been spared numerous car accidents, being hit by five drunk drivers to be specific, two others in which my car hydroplaned and never hit moving or stationary objects, and even more when you added in my Mom, Dad, Ned's and Corey's "near misses" over the years.

One such "miracle" was recalled over and over again throughout four decades following the sub-zero winter of 1983. After the Pizza Hut date, Ned began asking Daisy out regularly for dinner and/or dancing at the local establishments in town. Corey and I were only eight years old, but in the mid '80's, no one was getting arrested for leaving kids at home to brush their teeth and tuck themselves into bed. We were too poor for babysitters when I lived with Mom alone, but with us to keep one another company, what is the worst that could happen? (They came home once after only an hour and found us jumping on our twin beds in the dark laughing in the bedroom. We were mortified!)

After a few short months, they had gone on dates, spent time talking in one of their apartments, stayed up playing cards and telling stories. One December night, the temps were arctic in Chicagoland, and the pipes burst in our cold underground apartment. With the pipes all buried half underground since our first story brick 2-bedroom left us looking up to see out of the kitchen and bedroom windows, when the earth got cold, it was cold! That night, the kitchen sink pipe burst leaving water spraying all over the kitchen and into the living room carpeting. Well, the first call from Daisy to Ned left us with an invitation to have a "sleepover" down the way in their 2nd story apartment with solid pipes, dry carpeting, and toasty radiator heat to boot.

We packed a few scant items in a tiny overnight bag and trekked through the dark, our eyes tearing in the bitter winds, as we rushed down the sidewalk to their back steps. Sprinting up the stairs, we greeted the warm air ushering us into Apt 207. Corey was rubbing his eyes coming out of his bedroom wondering what was going on. It was after midnight after all and we were all in need of some much needed sleep. I found Ned's old olive green military sleeping bag with a freshly encased pillow lying on the floor in Corey's room, thanked him for letting us come over to sleep, and quickly scrambled under the thick zippered covers. Never one to stay up late, I have no recollection of what happened that night as I was out in seconds. Daisy unpacked her toiletries on the tiny sink with a mirrored medicine cabinet above the faucet. She was probably bashful and grateful for his hospitality but didn't want to make too much of it. She was not ready to open her heart up this wide to another man after 25 years with my father, since the tender age of 12 and a painful marriage, and drawn-out divorce.

Over the next two days while the pipes and water damage was repaired, Daisy's toothbrush sat next to Ned's in the medicine cabinet. He felt more and more prepared to think of his future not just as he and Corey against the world, but perhaps ready to say yes to a second marriage. They had been tragically abandoned by Corey's Mom who fled a few short months after Corey's birth, and so young he was not even able to say "Mama" yet. Ned had been the most steadfast and devoted father ever since. He provided everything Corey needed, did all of the shopping, cooking, chores, laundry, and was full-time Dad, Toolmaker by day and Mr. Mom by night.

Following two nights with "the girls" staying under his roof, then seeing the empty space where Daisy's toothbrush had temporarily resided next to his, Ned knew he wanted to take the plunge and ask Daisy to marry him. They could become one-third of the "Brady Bunch" and figure out somehow to merge two single parents with kids the same age and build a family in the winter of '84.

He found the perfect diamond ring set in 14K gold, with gold prongs and smaller stones surrounding the centered solitaire. Knowing that Corey and I had to be on the "same page", he talked things over with us letting us know that things were going to be much different in the future. My Mom and I would not have to hide our cereal in tupperware containers to protect our breakfast and pastas from the cockroaches and mice anymore. He was going to be certain of that. We were going to be a family, and Ned would take great care and provide for us. He had a very stable job of 20+ years at a tool and die company since being an apprentice fresh out of the National Guard. He worked extremely hard, took his position seriously, and was appropriately paid for his success. Daisy would now be a Mom to Corey, cooking, baking, sewing, and giving *lots* of hugs, which he was not at *all* used to. (Eewwwww!) Ned assured us that we would have a house of some sort, both kids would have their own rooms, we would take family vacations, and he would provide financial stability that my Mom and I lacked long before the divorce from my Dad.

We all had an enormous amount of healing to do as individuals. We experienced trauma as young children in the form of abuse, neglect, growing up too soon, divorce, betrayal of parents, and shattered hearts. But, there was hope. The beginning stages of healing took place when Ned and Daisy exchanged their vows on January 28th, 1984 in a little Methodist chapel on a cold Saturday afternoon in a tiny suburban church with only three witnesses. The pastor, Corey and I looked on as our parents promised to "have and to hold", "for richer and for poorer", "in sickness and in health", and "til death do us part." They signed the marriage license on that gray day on which Daisy donned a simple burgundy dress and heels with gold jewelry, and Ned in his shirt, straight tie, suit jacket over dress slacks and belt with polished black dress shoes. There was no fanfare, no pomp and circumstance, no musicians, no photographer or videographer, and nary a flower bouquet. Short, sweet, to the point, and vows were made that would last a lifetime. They would have to, with all they would face.

Chapter 8:   Racing through the night

January 20, 2023 - 1:45 am EST

Matthew 7:10 - "How much more will your Father in Heaven give good gifts to those who ask Him!"

"No! I knew it!" Ned shouted into the phone.

"I am calling you to tell you she is not talking like she was before. Her voice is much fainter and I don't know what this means.....I waited as long as I could, but I knew I had to call you to come right over."

Ned slammed the phone down in a mad rush to wake Corey on the couch, grab the car keys and speed mercilessly back to the hospital in Central Florida. The warmth of the evening was replaced by a balmy cool, in which the humidity hung in the air like cobwebs. It was thick. You could see and feel it and the air would adorn your face when rushing through the wet darkness. Ned was stunned in his heart at the unraveling events. He shook Corey awake, who had only slept a scarce 90 minutes since arriving from Texas. His flight landed at roughly 11 pm and he was forced to grab a shuttle to take him the 60 miles north to his Dad's house, knowing visiting hours had ended at the hospital already. Corey's previous day's 12-hour shift left his eyes bloodshot, legs fatigued, and his thoughts scattered. Crashing at least three hours on the couch would be required before facing Daisy's condition and what the following days might hold for them as a family.

Pushing past Ned's abrupt anger on the other end of the line, I returned my focus to my sweet Mom laying on the cool white sheets, moisture on her face from perspiration and her lips dry and creased. I stroked her head with a wet washcloth, massaged her hands gently, and applied lotion to her abdomen, burning from the electrode adhesive pads that were pulling at her skin. I only had a short time to know for sure that I presented the Gospel to my Mom before Ned and Corey arrived. I had no idea what emotional state they would be in and Jesus was not welcome in our conversations for years, so I had my moment. I had to take it.

"Mom, you said you believed in Jesus as a little girl. You have heard me talk about all He has done for me and James, Lilly and Marcus. You have seen the miracles He has done. He is a GOOD GOOD Father, and He came to earth just simply to lay His life down for you, to give His life for yours so you can be with Him forever. Unspeakable things were done to you. Every time you wept, He wept. When your heart broke, His heart broke. Mom, His Name is

Jesus, and you must choose Him. This is the only way. He wants to heal you, He loves you, you have to say 'Yes!' to Jesus."

She was so weak, her eyes going in and out from being open and focused, to drifting closed. Her breathing labored, and mostly steady, she would utter a few syllables here and there. She stopped reciting lines from the worship songs I had been singing over the past six hours and she grew more and more tired. Watching the monitors again, I laid hands gently on her abdomen, "Spirit of death, I rebuke you and you have NO dominion here! I plead the *Blood* of Jesus over my Mother, the Lord gave her LIFE, she is HIS! I speak Health and LIFE over her entire body, in the Name of Jesus, from the crown of her head to the soles of her feet and the trillions of cells in between. I declare she will live and not die and see the Goodness of God in the Land of the LIVING! In the Name of Jesus!"

My prayers were getting bolder, louder and more confident as negative evidence stared me in the face. Abraham never waivered nor doubted. Supernatural faith and strength surged through my entire body. I was being sustained by Heavenly means. (Friends at home praying saw an angel standing behind me putting both hands into my back simply a continual white glow and strength from Our Heavenly Father sent to uplift me through this battle, which I knew nothing of for days to come. Another angel in the room stood at the head of my Mom's bed wearing a bright red sash. Seeing this angel on only two occasions, it was surmised this was a salvation angel awaiting my Mom's decision to be indelibly written into the Lamb's Book of Life. These confirmations were a balm to my weary soul in the hours that followed our long stretch of sleepless days.)

I needed thirty seconds to text a fast message to James to pray for salvation and my Mom's decision to choose Jesus before the men arrived. James...

Chapter 9:   The Day After Prince Charming

Matthew 6:25, 27 - "Therefore I tell you, do not worry about your life...can any one of you by worrying add a single hour to your life?"

The next day after meeting James and Ryan, I went to work smelling like cigarettes, wearing all my same clothing after sleeping in my dress shirt and jeans, scrubbing my body as clean as it could get, but on 3 hours sleep and a commute to work, I had no time to pack a lunch or shower. Wetting my hair slightly without shampooing, would only serve to make me smell like an actively lit cigarette and draw a bunch more attention from customers and co-workers. It was already bad enough I would have to explain why the most virtuous girl in the store slept in her clothes after meeting her "knight in shining armor". Oh, boy. This was going to be one, long day.....

"Good morning, Cassie? How are you this morning?"

"Good, just tired...can I head out to the outside yard and fill the customer survey forms?" "Sure, just don't be too long, you need to get to the head cash register before the doors unlock in 12 minutes."

"Okay, I will be quick!" I liked to say good morning to all the yard guys at Menards, be cheerful and brighten up the day. Besides, I could *never* sit still, so walking for a ½ mile or more to start the shift was better than if I just stood at my register for 6-8 hours with only two bathroom breaks and a 30-minute lunch break.

"What's up, Cass? We never saw you again after you started talking to blondie last night," Mark chided.

"Oh, yeah, I know. Sorry! Thanks for inviting me out with you guys. My friend from high school called and she came out to play darts and I never even saw you guys again. Sorry! I didn't mean to blow you off."

"That's cool. Oh, man, you reek, Girl. What's up?" He said, catching a whiff of my bar clothes from the night before.

"I know, I have never smoked a day in my life, now I am like a walking Marlboro. It's so embarrassing. Well, maybe I'll have a good story to tell out of it, so I guess I'll make the best of it. Have a great day, Mark! See ya later."

"Yeah, see ya," Mark echoed with a confused look on his face.

Knowing I had no break for 4 hours to close my eyes, no money for lunch, really, and I would be tired and hungry, this would have been a good time in my life to know the Lord and to pray! I didn't really grasp at all what praying was about back then, so I probably sucked it up, pinched myself every now and then, and splashed cold water on my makeupless face as often as possible.

All I could talk about the *entire* day long was James. James, James, James. The girls in the wallcoverings department told me I was delusional. The two 50-year-olds who worked in electrical thought my story sounded "nice" but we will have to see if anything comes of it. The other cashiers were young high school and college kids who I didn't say much to, and then there were the sweet Indian mothers I worked with from 8:00-5:00 pm all summer long, and they told me cute stories about their kids while we worked. Charanjit was the "Mama Hen" I spent the most time confiding in. She was savvy, competitive, determined, and boy did she know how to get her way. I knew convincing her James was a decent guy would be a hard sell, but long about 10 am I got up the guts to spill my story and see if it stuck.

"So, last night something really crazy happened," I divulged.

"Jes?" She said in her thick Punjabi accent.

"I went next door with Mark and some guys and started playing darts. Then, Belle joined me and, well, we were playing a game of Cricket for a while when two guys in their early 20's came in to play, too. There was only 1 board open and ours so they asked us to play a round."

"And?" She rushed me to share the details, rotating her hand in a circular motion.

"And, well, there was this really cute guy with blond hair named James, and we stayed and talked from around 10 pm until 2 am! I have never stayed out late in my life, never talked to a *stranger*, and my Mom doesn't even know this stuff yet. It is like the craziest thing I've ever done. I stayed awake thinking about him, and woke up thinking about him, and now I am so ridiculously tired, but I don't care, because I met him and I think he seems amazing!"

"Cassandra, dear, jou know that hez probly not the boy your parents want you marrying, no?" she asked in her thick Punjabi accent.

"I don't know. I am not sure. He seemed so *real*. We talked about church, songs we like, our families, his Mom, the farm he grew up on, he just seemed so *honest*. I don't meet a lot of guys like that."

"Sweetheart, just take one day at zee time. ONE day," she smiled while emphasizing one, like I couldn't let my head be up floating in the clouds.

"Thanks, yeah, I know," I paused, "Thank you for listening."

The day seemed long, and I couldn't wait to get home. I drove home in a sleep-deprived daze, forgetting how I ultimately arrived there safely. All I could think of was first getting some sleep and then spilling the story to my

mom. She was my best friend and I told her absolutely *everything*.

I stripped the cream-colored Sears, long-sleeved work shirt off and

men's denim stonewashed jeans. I dumped them and the filthy socks straight

into the washing machine which I would run with my dirty laundry after

showering. I showered in the longest, hottest, shower I could bear until fatigue

got the best of me. Climbing into my green comforter and soft, cool, clean

sheets, I slept straight through dinner and just shy of golden hour.

"Sweetie, sweetie?" Mom called from the bedroom doorway. "Why

didn't you come down to dinner? Are you feeling okay?"

"Yes, I needed sleep after staying at Belle's last night, and I should

have explained more to you guys about why I stayed in town and needed to

nap after work. Sorry, I didn't call you at work to give you a heads up," I

apologized.

"I was a little worried since this isn't like you. Anyway, we have chicken

chalupa on the counter still warm for you for dinner when you're ready."

"Did you make it with the jalapeno peppers again, Mom? You know I'm

a lightweight when it comes to spicy foods."

"Oh, just a *little* bit of the peppers and a lot of orange juice to sweeten it up and dull the fire. You'll love it!"

"Do you want to hear about last night? I met...someone."

"Oh?" she asked coyly, a smile curling up at the corners of her mouth.

"Mom, don't be so dramatic. Yes, well, his name is.....let me just show you his card," I replied, fishing the business card out of my back right pocket. "He was nice, funny, and honest and seemed so genuine. Here's his business card he gave me." I displayed the card so she could read it in the dimming sunlight in the kitchen.

"James McKnight, Energy Specialist. Wow, Cassandra McKnight has *such* a nice ring to it!"

"Mom, I *just* met him! Besides, it was in a bar and that is never a good sign. I was just hanging out with Belle watching the Bulls 3-peat and he just happened to walk in with his best friend, Ryan, who is getting married in June. I have absolutely no idea if I will ever see him or talk to him ever again. I have to drive back to school for graduation this weekend, and pack and bring all of my things home and I don't have time for this distraction right now."

"Sounds like a nice distraction, " she chided.

"I have no idea. I will see if he ever comes into the store to find me. I gave him no phone number, the town I live in, nothing to go off of, so if he wants to pursue me, Menards is his only shot. Now, how about some dinner? I am famished after skipping breakfast and having 3 pieces of stale white bread Belle's Mom had stashed in the kitchen. Not a good nutritional day at all. I'll eat and then go workout, Mom, if that's okay. What are you two up to tonight?"

"Oh you know, the usual. I just finished gardening, and I need to do some housework and maybe a game of Scrabble," she said romantically.

"Oh, brother, you guys are so weird. Scrabble? Mom, you're like, not even 50, so why does your life make you sound old? You're gorgeous, energetic, fun, and you guys need friends to hang out with!" I said, rolling my eyes.

"Cassie, now it's you who is being dramatic...it's Thursday night and I get up at 6 to go to work, or have you forgotten about adult responsibilities?"

"True," I conceded. "But you guys have to get a life on Fridays and Saturdays!"

"Alright, enough...enjoy the chicken and have a great workout. I hope you're thankful I found this place for you while you were away at school."

"Yeah, I love Women's Workout World because there are no weird guys there ogling you while you're sweaty and half-naked. That's just gross."

"Enjoy, I'll see you when you come home to shower. I'll say goodnight before we go to bed."

"Okay, love you, Mom!"

"I love you too, Sweetie. To the moon and back."

That flashed me inadvertently back into the present moment. I love you, to the Moon and back....she said. We just sat in the hospital room, holding hands, I was praying, reciting these Heavenly song lyrics, and telling each other we love one another, forgive each other, and now she can barely whisper. Lord, what is happening? Please let her sleep, get rest, and be fueled with energy to fight these organs shutting down. She needs sleep *first*, then water, food, but mostly, she needs You! I am going to keep praying, laying hands on her and rebuking the devourer. Nothing is keeping her from fulfilling all you have planned for her life.

I went back to praying, praising and watching the monitors. When her blood pressure would plummet to 80/30, I would lay hands on her, cancel the assignment of death off her body and speak LIFE over her body, soul, mind and spirit and watch the numbers spike back to 100/50. This happened over and over all night, over a 6-hour time span. The Lord is here and He is answering! I will continue to pray and hold the line of faith in this place. We are alone so NO doubt, unbelief or fear can enter here. I will not repeat the bad medical report. No words that align with death will come off my lips! Lord, you gave me dominion here and I am calling on your infinite power!

Chapter 10:   Where is my Knight in Shining Armor?

Matthew 7:7- "Ask and it will be given to you, seek and you will find, knock and the door will be opened to you. For everyone who asks receives, the one who seeks finds, and to the one who knocks, the door will be opened."

It was nearing the end of May 1996, almost three weeks had passed, and there were no James sightings. I grew restless of him not coming through the 10-foot tall sliding glass doors at Menards each day that I worked, Monday through Friday. I had his number, but I didn't want him to think I was stalking him. I talked about him to my co-workers, to Belle, to my parents, and to myself. I imagined his dreamy blue eyes and wondered how I could have chosen to not give him my number? Because, duh, you just went through an intense breakup of an engagement relationship lasting three long years. That's why. Oh yeah, I reasoned. I was being guarded, cautious. Isn't that the wise thing to do, wait until your heart begins to heal before you dive into another romantic attachment? Yes. That is wise. Relationship experts and my therapist, Mary, would have said that, too. My Psych professors at college would echo the same sentiments. Until there is time and space to understand who you are after the trauma of a broken engagement, and you know what type of husband you are seeking, do not do anything rash or hasty. But, I am 21 years old and I am not getting any younger! My friends are engaged at college, some are getting married this weekend after graduation, and Belle has had a boyfriend for two years. (I cannot stand his guts. He is a jerk and treats her like she's expendable.)

God, will I ever find the right husband? Now, I am damaged goods, used, discarded and thrown out by this man I thought was going to be my husband. We picked out childrens' names together, knew where we would settle and we would belong to his family's Lutheran Church. I converted to Lutheranism just to marry him after all! I learned the liturgy, went to six adult conversion classes, read books on Martin Luther and memorized the Catechism. I cannot believe I spent three years with this family of 40 people, 7 siblings, 18 nieces and nephews, dinners, holidays, family summer vacations at the cottage. Now, here I am, rejected right before the wedding and my penultimate college graduation. The timing of this heartbreak could not have been worse. Studying four full years and keeping a 4.0 GPA has been the hardest, most stressful and tumultuous feat I have ever accomplished. There is nothing like taking a deep breath and waiting to exhale for 8 long semesters. Pouring over books, forsaking all fun and socializing, and being married to textbooks and study caroles had taken a toll on my identity and my perspective. I had no joy and life was all about the all-consuming pursuit of the perfect 4.0 GPA and graduating with highest honors from a prestigious university.

So, now that I was achieving this on Sunday, why wasn't I happy? Because I am a jilted bride, I thought. Well, not jilted, at least I wasn't dumped at the altar like those Jerry Springer episodes. It sure felt the same, however. Anyway, where was I? Oh, yeah. James. Did he like me? Was he attracted to me or interested in coming in to see me and at least talking? I mean, we talked for, like, 5 hours a few weeks ago. Sigh.

I guess there is only one way to find out. Go back to the place it all began. Today's Wednesday and another $1.00 drink night. I bet Belle will be up for another Bull's Game and some darts. But, if I call her, she will be all up in my face about "the surfer guy", as she referred to James, and be nosey and her same Belle self. Did I want to get that kind of static?

No, I'll ask the guys from work to walk over with me and then I will just aimlessly walk through the bar looking for him, but look like I am *not* looking for him. That's brilliant. Okay, now, I need to pack quickly, if I'm gonna look like a real girl after a long sweaty day at the store!

I quickly grabbed the spaghetti-strapped denim dress my Grandma Mueller just bought me this month with a cute, white short-sleeved t-shirt to go underneath with a pair of sandals and my makeup bag. I stuffed things into my purple backpack with some food for lunch, a $5.00 bill and my keys. Scarfing down some oatmeal for breakfast, I kissed my Mom good-bye and headed off to the store to open for the day. Nervous energy surged through my veins at the anticipatory thought of running into James again after work!

The day seemed to drag by with some fun and generous customers at the return counter. The other hoity-toity housewife types that demanded every penny back on something they bought last week now listed in this Saturday's sale ad weren't as pleasant. I mindlessly counted change for customers, indicated where departments are located in the store, told the 20th customer where to find the bathroom, and it still wasn't 5 o'clock! Why was this day dragging by so slowly? What was that adage my Mom was telling me since before I could ride a tricycle? Oh, yes. "A watched pot never boils!" She would say with sage wisdom. "The more you wait, the longer it will take, Cassandra. Just go do something else," she would advise. Good advice, Mom, but easier said than done.

Just as I got into the swing of having a better attitude about waiting, it was quarter-to-five and I was just about to wrap up my shift, count my cash drawer, and go change clothes. The paint (wallcoverings) guys agreed to walk over with me so I didn't appear to be some "nerd" getting dressed up and walking into a bar alone like a sitting duck. That is *never* a good plan! You just get bad pick-up lines and feel like you've been talking to a sleazy used car salesman.

Punching out with my name badge, I headed to the far rear of the store with my backpack to change into my dress and sandals. I applied all new, fresh makeup after washing my face with a washcloth and some lukewarm water. I was in too much of a rush to wait for it to get hot, right? As soon as my mascara was crisp, cheeks dusted with some powdered blush, and lip gloss was on, I ran my brush urgently through my hair the obligatory 50 strokes, give or take. One last glance said I was ready!

Lost in thought for a moment, I reflected on the night I met James. I was mortified! I was like a cute, in shape athletic girl who lost her mind and put on clothing that 100% did *not* match my physique. I cannot believe my ex-fiance convinced me to wear men's work shirts and high top shoes all those months. While I looked like Sporty Spice, which was a cute vibe for some, it just wasn't natural for me. I enjoyed the privilege of wearing dresses, jewelry and light makeup to emulate the femininity of my mother. She modeled it well, and although I felt so uncomfortable embracing femininity for much of my years, I desired someday to be a grateful wife and my greatest passion was to be a mother. Tonight, I actually look like a girly girl! I hoped James would be there.

Dashing to the front sliding exit doors, I saw the paint department guys congregating around Mark's car and Mike, Chris and the others were with him. I accepted the short ride next door to avoid walking across the expansive parking lot and grassy berm which could soak my sandals with mud-drenched ground due to recent May rain.

I didn't talk much on the quick drive as I was still formulating what I was going to say if and when I saw "him". Gulp. I swallowed hard with my tongue and lips feeling suddenly intensely dry at the thought of seeing James. Would he remember me? Would he want to talk? I guess it was about time I found out the answer to my myriad questions.

We lined up at the door where they were waving cover charges for women again since "$1 drink night" is designed to bring in the masses on Wednesdays. The fog above peoples' heads accompanied with the beer sign neon lights reflecting off the hazy atmosphere made it difficult to identify distinct faces from a distance. I said a furtive "Thanks, have fun," to the Menards gang and began surreptitiously looking for James's blond locks. I remembered details about his appearance to be seeking out: he is 5 inches taller, has blond hair, mesmerizing blue eyes, an athletic build and he has a propensity to wear a t-shirt with denim shorts. This will help me ID him in the bustling crowd. Shoulders were glancing off me left and right, everywhere I turned my head, looking for this mystery man. For minutes, I walked around the main bar in counterclockwise circles, looking carefully at every face around the dart boards, all six pool tables, towards the back where the video games were perched, and into the side room near the bathrooms. I took a deep breath, exhaling slowly, thinking, "Cassie, you are really desperate. This is ridiculous." I was determined to look once more around the main floor where the majority of the patrons were talking, drinking, laughing, yelling, smoking, and telling loud jokes. This time, walking clockwise in my leather buckled sandals, I took careful steps so as to not let my bare toes be crushed under the shoes and boots of these lewd strangers.

For a girl who hates smoke, drugs, and alcohol, what on earth was I doing here? I don't like drinking, I don't like all of this yelling and swearing, and what on earth would I want to look for a boyfriend or husband in a place like this? Maybe I should just walk next door to my car and get a good night's sleep.

Walking clockwise on the outside of the main crowd, I spotted what could have been James's blond locks now facing away from me while he was slowly advancing towards me, in a counterclockwise direction. His right shoulder almost brushed past my right, when I reached to gently put four fingers on his collarbone, saying, "Hi. Uh, James.........right?" I faked belatedly pulling his name out of my archives. I pulled it off, surprisingly and I sounded like I was just formulating his name yet was thinking about him, constantly.

"Yeah! Cassie! I thought you might be here."

He came to see me? Sweat began welling up under my arms as my face flushed red with excitement. "You did? Oh, well, yeah, I guess that makes sense. It's Wednesday and the Bulls are playing! Is Ryan here, or who are you with?"

"No, I came alone. I was looking for you. Wanna play some darts?"

And there it was. He was thinking about me these past three weeks as I was thinking of him! That's amazing! He didn't blow me off. He wasn't being rude. He even came back to look for me twenty-one days later. What was I going to say, and how could I keep it cool so he didn't know I have been obsessed with him and thinking of and talking about him, incessantly, to all who would listen?

"Sure. I don't have any quarters though, so...."

"I've got it. It's on me. You grab a board, and I'll go make change." What a gentleman!

"Good manners, chivalrous, my Mom and Grandma just might approve, " I immediately reasoned. "Cassie, don't blow it, this guy is actually interested in you and he's the first "hot guy" you have even looked at since the breakup! *Stay cool!*" I instructed myself.

"You look great, by the way. I like your dress," James complimented.

"Oh, thanks! My Grandma took me shopping for graduation and bought it for me just a few weeks ago. She's my favorite person on earth and I just love wearing it and thinking about her. Glad I look more, um, you know, human since the last time I saw you!"

"Dumb, dumb, just relax! Why did you even say that?" I admonished myself.

Coming back with quarters, James pulled out his set of darts from home. (He had come prepared to play!) "Well, that's cool you have an awesome Grandma, I have two that I am close to and see all the time. We have Sunday dinners after church with my Mom's family and have been eating out at the farm almost every week all through farming season. Off season, we see them a little less, but we can walk across the road to visit them anytime. My other Grandma and Grandpa are in town a few miles away, and we see them every month for every birthday and holiday."

"That's amazing! I love close-knit families," I answered, quickly.

"So, do you wanna shoot first?" James politely asked, bringing my attention back to the dartboard. He gently extended the three darts towards my right hand.

"Okay," I said nervously, retrieving the darts from his left hand as my fingers lightly brushed against his. Last time, I just met him and had no idea that I would actually now be playing him one-on-one where there was more pressure, the stakes were higher, and the shaking in my knees would be more apparent in a flimsy cotton denim dress than in my thick Levis. I took a deep breath, planted my right toes at the line, turning sideways to the left, positioned my thumb and forefinger securely on the shaft of the dart and bending my elbow, shot an arrow at the 16, then missed the 15, and shot again at 16 missing wide. "Well, at least I pointed," I thought. It wasn't a total bust!

"Nice start," he complimented.

Next, I was not prepared for what happened. He boldly pulled all three darts out of the plastic honey-combed board from the wild pattern I threw and confidently retreated back to the line. He stood eye level to the Bull's Eye, toed the line, bent his knees and elbow, standing at a strategic angle that showed he had done this hundreds of times before. I surveyed his physique, and noticed his muscular torso and forearms, and oh my, did he look amazing in those jeans. I couldn't believe this kind, sensitive and sexy guy was actually asking me to play darts with him!

He made short work of the round, pointing two or three darts and allowing me to retrieve them for my turn. I have no idea how many times I missed that night, but the conversation flowed easily, my ankle-lengthed, thin blue dress waving in the breeze as I briskly walked to the board and back numerous times, joking, flirting, and making small talk. The hours flew by, he won handily, and I realized he was probably sandbagging us a few weeks prior so he didn't obliterate the very girl he was hitting on, mortifying her on the very first night.

As the dart games wound down, we found a way to end the conversation for the night. Being sensible adults, we both knew to drive home at a reasonable hour this time and obtain the much needed sleep before a full

shift at work the next morning. James slyly inquired, "So, are you going to give

me your number this time?"

"My number, how about we go on a date instead?" I blurted before I

knew it.

What was I saying! It just vomited out of my mouth before I even

thought about what I was saying! How is this possible! Cassie, you are

ridiculous. Let *him* make the first move. Didn't your Grandma tell you that a

hundred thousand times in your life already?

"Woah...okay, I didn't know you were that kind of girl!" he said,

amused.

"Um, I'm not, what kind? Nevermind. I will be glad to give you my

phone number but I don't have a business card. As you know, I am graduating

in 3 days, looking for a full time job, and then I will be a bonafide adult, too," I

said, recovering from my stammering. I wrote my parents' home number on

the back of a napkin and placed it into his hand while blushing profusely.

Gaining boldness, I plunged ahead, "If you were willing to drive here

alone tonight to look for me, why did you wait three whole weeks? You know where I work. What made you wait so long?" The question hung in the air and I waited with suspense for his answer.

"That's easy, since you didn't know if I was a serial killer, I ran home in the cold not dressed for the weather and I caught a cold and have been sick ever since. I just got over it, and headed out tonight since it's Wednesday. May I walk you to your car?"

"My car? Oh, yes, my car! I am parked next door, I came from work with some friends and they drove me over. I can walk, it's okay."

"Are you sure? Do you still think I'm dangerous?" he asked, laughing.

"No, no, it's not like that. It will be good to take a moment in the cool air before my drive home. It's about a half-hour and it will feel good to walk a bit. This was really fun. I cannot thank you enough. Thanks for the games."

Awkward smiles ensued, no hugs, no kisses, no handshakes, he walked me to the door and out into the brisk, moonlit Spring night. He placed his hand on my back as he guided me carefully through the crowd, protecting me. At the sensation of him touching my back, it felt like his skin was burning a hole in my dress! Wow, there was so much warmth in his touch and in the night itself.

"Good night, James. I hope to talk to you soon." I said cheerfully, waving and walking north across the grass that seemed so concerningly muddy hours earlier and now was not even the faintest thought in my mind.

He smiled and said, "Good night!"

The drive home is not even a memory in my mind. How I made it the 15 miles home through all of the twists and turns, I will never recall. However, the fantasy-like thoughts swimming through my mind entertained me through the winding and hilly roads, passing forest preserves and open pastures before ultimately reaching my parents' subdivision in a bustling suburb of Chicago.

I raced up the 16-step straight staircase at the foyer of their 2-story home and threw myself onto my bed with sheer delight and stars in my eyes. Kicking off my sandals and gently lifting my dress and t-shirt off my sun-bathed arms I smiled, dreaming of my life as Cassandra McKnight. It did have a good ring to it! Throwing on pajamas, brushing my teeth, washing my face, and then hurrying into my green bedroom, I allowed the moonlight to sing me to sleep as I dreamed of all things James.

Chapter 11:   Life with James

Romans 8:5 - "Those who live according to the flesh have their minds set on what the flesh desires, but those who live in accordance with the Spirit have their minds set on what the Spirit desires."

The next two years were a whirlwind of going out with James, working full-time at a manufacturing company while James still flourished in his managerial role at a local family-owned energy business. He was climbing the ranks and so was I. We were paying off college debt, enjoying an occasional dinner out to celebrate a promotion or new role at work, and getting together with friends from college we both knew. I loved Ryan and his wife, Elizabeth, and we got together every so often for double dates. I saw less and less of Belle as my relationship with James was based on very different things than her lifestyle with her boyfriend. Also, our full-time jobs, my college classes for my Purchasing Manager license, going to our new church, and thinking ahead to the future was consuming so much of my time.

Dates consisted of going rolling blading, taking an occasional romantic walk around the lake nearby, bike rides, playing tennis or racquetball, and lots of time watching TV prime time shows that were all the rage in the late 1990's. Thursday nights were full of Seinfeld, Friends, Frazier and ER. We knew every quotable line from each comedy and got attached to the dramatic heart-pumping action of the medical drama that stole America's heart. The months flew by in our young adult lives as we worked hard, saved a lot of cold hard cash for whatever the future held, and enjoyed being young and getting super fit. Going to the gym, lifting, getting lean and strong, and taking turns spotting with our mutual friend, Greg, filled our weeknights. Weekends were for football and basketball games on TV, Sunday afternoon reading and napping on the couch for me (to catch up on sleep from long weeks as a Senior Purchasing Agent), and cheating on our strict diets by ordering CPA deep dish spinach and mushroom pizzas.

One hot Summer July night immediately following work, I drove home with the windows down enjoying the humid breeze. I was sweltering in the heat and looking forward to at least getting in a good workout before dousing myself in a cold shower to cool down. Getting home to the apartment, I changed into a t-shirt and shorts, ankle socks and white dingy gym shoes when James walked in and dropped his keys on the counter.

"You're home early! That's so great. I was hoping to get a workout in and then cool down in the shower. I sweated through every layer of clothing on the way home and my leather seats were even wet when I got out of the car. I'm so gross right now," I over shared with James as he walked in.

"Yeah, traffic was super light tonight. I'll go with you. Let me throw on some clothes," he replied.

As he pulled on and laced up his shoes, I grabbed water and a book to read on the elliptical. I looked longingly at his super handsome face and curly blond locks in the humid July air and boldly inquired, "Will you marry me?"

James' gaze lingered on my face, glowing with slight perspiration and paused, turned around slowly and walked over to his nightstand. Sliding open a cabinet door, he pulled out a small red velvet box. He held the box up in front of me, walking nearer and opened it in the shadowy sunlight streaming in through the blinds.

"What? Right here? Right now? Oh my! When did you buy this? How long have you had it hidden in there?"

In James' common way of communicating, he said very little and did not attempt to answer my barrage of questions. He leaned over, placed the diamond on my ring finger and smiled his dimpled smile.

I do not remember all of what I said next, but I remember giving him an extremely hard time for never asking me to marry him, not getting on one knee, and no sappy lines of commitment. Regretting that I was sweaty and dressed to workout instead of wearing fancy clothes at an upscale restaurant or on a romantic getaway, I waited to see what he would say or do next. I believe I was jumping up and down and excitedly saying, "This is so gorgeous! How did you know what to buy for me?"

"Let's go celebrate. Let's go to Chevy's."

"Like this, all sweaty and...," I trailed off.

"Let's clean up, get ready and eat at our favorite place to celebrate the beginning of our engagement," James said pragmatically.

"Wow, this day sure turned around in a hurry! Okay....I'll be as quick as I can!"

"Take your time. I'll go use the guest bathroom and wait in the living room."

We drove to our favorite place, Chevy's Mexican Restaurant, where we had eaten several times before. They generously offered unlimited homemade tortilla chips, great ambiance, Spanish music, tiled tables, and friendly waitstaff. On a Monday night, there was no waitlist and we were immediately seated in a sunset facing section.

"Wow, this is so incredible. I need to pinch myself. I waited so long for this day, to share this news with our friends and family and celebrate me becoming Mrs. James McKnight! I am in a dream right now....make sure I am really awake!"

James snuck to tell the waitress about our celebration so they could deliver a free surprise ice cream delicacy for dessert to our table. It was a fun and memorable evening. We had myriad plans to make over the next many months for our wedding, our future, our family, our first house, and this was only just the beginning.

On May 22, 1999, we were married in a small chapel inside a Methodist Church in the Northwest suburbs of Chicago on a cool and rainy Saturday morning. Over one hundred and twenty family and friends came to wish us well, blow bubbles, listen to our vows, and hear First Corinthians 13 and Ecclesiastes 4:12 read over us by two dear friends, Ryan and Ramona (my closest girlfriend from college). We danced the hours away until the sun began to wane in the sky over the green manicured golf course lawn just outside the expansive glass wall of windows. James' best man, Dave, a surgeon from Arizona gave the toast, Ned danced the Daddy-Daughter dance with me, we laughed, and talked so much we forgot to eat and enjoy our champagne toast. We greeted every grandparent, cousin, aunt, uncle, parent and friend as we traveled table to table, hugging, laughing and enjoying the festivities. The day was a joyful blur as we forgot to get several Mueller family pictures in our rush to enjoy the moment. We tried to bless everyone with conversation, give hugs and offer a quick dance to dozens of guests. Once the three-tiered white wedding cake was eaten, and crumbs left behind on the white linen tablecloths, the DJ began wrapping up with the last song. He played "The Last Dance" by Donna Summer and the last guests said their farewells to the new Mr. and Mrs. James McKnight and drove home.

Since we had chosen to pay for our own wedding on a very frugal budget, our 10 am wedding and noon luncheon reception was not only spectacular and affordable, but we now had free time between dinner and midnight to enjoy with our closest friends.

"So, James and I want to take the 8 of you out to celebrate...the night is too young, our enthusiasm is high, and we can't stop the party this soon! We are taking you all to Chevy's in Schaumburg to celebrate...our treat. Let's go!"

James walked me to his waiting '90 Burgundy Mustang, and helped me slowly lift my wedding gown, although bustled, carefully into the car. The last thing I wanted was for stains from dirty rainwater or door hinge grease to mar the white satin gown. Dave and their high school friends hopped in his rental car while my cousin, Ramona and her hubby, Ryan and Elizabeth piled into Ryan's SUV.

Meeting at Chevy's less than twenty minutes later, we got a table for ten on the veranda, and sat until the sun eclipsed the buildings and a Spring May chill settled onto our sun-scorched arms and legs. The realization that this was the 3-year anniversary of our second "chance encounter" that Wednesday night at Chessie's settled on me. Remembering the wild temperature shift from sun-up to sun-down was reminiscent of James running home and catching cold for weeks on end after our first meeting.

"So, you guys, do you remember in '96 when James and I met at the bar, and he asked me for a ride?" I reminisced.

"Like, dude, what were you thinking asking a strange girl to let you get into her car the first day you met her! Duh, that was a deal killer, man," Joe piped up, James' other best friend since the seventh grade.

"Well, I guess it worked out for me after all, huh?" James quipped, stating the obvious.

"You're lucky, Bro. Cassie is *totally* out of your league, Jay," Dave commended, not missing an opportunity to "dis" his long-time best friend.

"Yeah, she is gorgeous, smart, and did you see her Mom? She is so hot! You know what they say, "Look at the mother if you wanna know what you're marrying!" Joe piped up.

"You guys are ridiculous! Yes, my Mom is smokin' for her age, but this is *my* wedding day, can you guys stop staring at her and flirting for, like, one day? I mean, reallllllyy. Just 'cuz you're single, that is gross!" I said, eyes blazing.

"Relax, Cass, I'm just saying, if Ned weren't around, you know, me and your Mom....."

"Alright, enough, I'm gonna throw up before I even *order* dinner let alone try to eat it....let's change the conversation. You guys are over the top, " I warned our buddies, jovially.

Dave picked up his water glass, ice jangling as he lifted it, and pronounced, "I would like to make a toast. To Mr. and Mrs. James McKnight, may you both enjoy many memories for years to come and have a spectacular honeymoon!" He winked at us and reached to clink glasses with the gang.

A cacophony of responses came as a reply to his toast in the form of, "Cheers!"

"Cheers, you two!

"Cheers!"

"Cheers for the years!"

"Cheers, congratulations!"

"We love you guys!"

They clinked their glasses while we performed the obligatory bride and groom smooch behind a cloth napkin.

Sitting out on the patio as the sun was beginning to set, we binged on the perfectly salted, fresh and warm all-you-can eat tortilla chips and drank pitchers of Blue Agave margaritas until it was time to drive to the O'hare airport hotel. The ATA flight was departing before 5 am to Cancun, Mexico.

Dave and Joe offered to take us to the hotel and drop our car at the apartment parking lot so we didn't have to keep it in long-term airport parking all week. My parents offered to pick us up from next Saturday night's return flight to celebrate our wedding and honeymoon with them and James' folks at their home.

This was all beginning to be so real and so invigorating! After a tumultuous childhood, moving over six times, changing custodial parents several times, living with Grandma Marie, and then wondering if I would ever find someone to love me after a failed engagement, my life was finally taking off. God had heard and answered many prayers, and I had no idea that He was going to use James and our lives together to take me from an abundantly insecure, fearful, perfectionistic, selfish, feminist girl and transform her into a Bride of Christ, purely adorned and living rightly for Him and only Him.

Chapter 12: The Honeymoon is Over

May 2001 - Chevy's, Schaumburg, IL (2nd anniversary)

Ephesians 4:31-32 - "Get rid of all bitterness, rage and anger, brawling and slander, along with every form of malice. Be kind and compassionate to one another, forgiving each other, just as in Christ God forgave you."

James ordered his favorite Mexican meal at our favorite place, where we went several times on carefree dates during the early years when life was light-hearted and fun, no stress of commitments, bills, marriage and disagreements. We celebrated the night of our unusual engagement, where I was pushy and impatient asking James to marry me, instead of the other way around. Little did I know that taking timelines into my own hands, forcing the engagement, manipulating events, and demanding my own way would pave the way for sorrow, pain, loneliness and isolation like I had never known in 25 years on earth.

We stared in silence across the table from one another, me pretending to actually read the menu through my eyes which were welling with tears. I didn't know what to say. How did we get here in 24 short months after what seemed to be a blissful adventure of planning a wedding, buying our dream house in a Chicago suburb, getting married and both of our fledgling careers taking off. We were two radically different people with polar opposite personalities and ways of conflict management, that is how. We ignored the pastor who did the Meyers-Briggs personality profile on us during premarital counseling and we got married despite what the statistics predicted. Determined to beat the odds, and be stubborn about "never getting divorced" since no one in our families either did (James' for the most part), or no one had a healthy long-lasting marriage to speak of in mine (that I knew of). We were in a standoff of silence and "friendship" that was neither intimate nor romantic. All of those Hollywood movies lied to hook women in with tantalizing fantasies of the knight in shining armor coming to sweep the damsel in distress off her feet and then they lived happily ever after. (Blah blah blah blah, gag.)

For 25 years, I was obsessed with soap operas, watched cheesy movies like "Serendipity", "Say Anything", and "Jerry Maguire" believing that the damaged girl with a painful past *could* marry the "boy next door" and have them ride off into the sunset together. How could we possibly have gotten to be total strangers in the same house, co-existing, paying the bills, going about our lives, and being so miserable, isolated, and lonely?

During these two years, I cried more times than I could count and left my Mom out of the "sounding board" role since I was too ashamed to admit how hard marriage had turned out to be. We dated three years after all and had our fair share of disagreements, misunderstandings, and hurt feelings. Somehow, we believed we should still get married. Now, we are staring at the back of one another's menus going through the motions of "celebrating" our anniversary.

"Do you know what you want?" Carmen, our waitress, had returned to take our order. "I want a husband who loves me!" I wanted to shout. "Um, I will have my usual taco salad, please. No guacamole. Thank you," I answered solemnly.

"And you, senor?" James was so deliberately slow at ordering and it drove me absolutely insane as I watched him stare, and pause, and ask questions, and then request the server's suggestions. Sigh. Does he realize they have other tables to wait on? Seriously? These people are so busy!

"I will have the steak burrito with beans and rice. And a horchata, please," he said about as somberly as I had.

"Si, Senor, I will put your orders in right away! Would you like more chips?"

We looked at each other as if determining whether or not this was a good idea.

"Sure, why not. Thank you," James broke the silence.

I tried to make small talk for a few minutes as we stared around the restaurant, people watching. I have no idea to this day what he could have possibly been thinking or feeling during these strained conversations, nor do I truly wish to know, if I am being honest with myself. The pain was just too intense for me as I stumbled upon a conversation topic I thought might entice him to respond with more than one word answers, yet I kept failing.

"Fine, I give up," I thought. We will just have this be like any other night, and instead of truly "talking" we will just exist like two people on a horrible first date, who cannot wait to say good-night, yet instead, we are stuck living in the same house with each other, and oh yeah, we're married. Gulp. Now what do we do?

The meal came quickly, yet not quickly enough, and I began moving my fork around my plate, not having an appetite due to the emotional stress. I forced myself to eat some, and then plunged forward into a topic of which I cannot recall. James' reply will live on in my memory forever.

"Don't talk or you'll ruin it."

I wanted to run from the table and weep in the car in solitude. How could he be so cold? Ruin dinner or ruin our marriage? How can not talking make anything better? That's our problem! We don't talk about the right things or in the right way. Honestly, I don't know. It's just a complete total and utter mess is what it is, and I don't know anyone who can help us. (I began to problem-solve silently instead of asking myself what I was doing to contribute to the problem.)

"Maybe going to church would help us. I wonder if he will go with me again. Perhaps a pastor can help," I ruminated in my mind.

We attended church the whole time we were engaged and found a church to be married in. Then, we attended for another several months until we bought our first house which was located 60 minutes away from the church. And that was that. No more church.

The drive home from the restaurant was filled with silent tension. I climbed out of the car in the garage, slipped off my heels at the back door and stole up to the bedroom to change for an early bedtime. I flopped on the bed and cried and cried until I couldn't remember thinking about anything else but the sadness. I must have finally fallen asleep.

"The train is coming, get out of the way!!!!!" someone shouted. James stepped onto the tracks and the train barrelled right for him and if he didn't get off the tracks soon, he was going to get.....

I woke up with a start, heart pounding, and mind racing. What happened? Where was James? Did he die? I woke from the nightmare before the train crushed him to pieces. Surely, he would not have been able to survive. Is that what I wanted? For him to be gone? Why would I dream of something so awful? Was I so demoralized by the state of our marriage that I would rather have it be over than try to resolve this immeasurable anguish? That cannot be the answer. I felt relief at the thought of no more pain and no divorce yet was ashamed my mind would conjure a dream of that nature after the emotional night we had endured. Surely, the pain of so much rejection by my Dad, Mom, other family members, and my former fiance coupled with the pain of abandonment left me scarred and traumatized. The years of counseling had only scratched the surface to reveal how wounded I was. I was overly sensitive and easily offended. (Looking back, I see this was enormous pride masking itself as insecurity and feeling unlovable. I would be so easily hurt by anything James would do or say, or fail to do. My expectations were completely unrealistic.)

122

We can't go on like this, there must be something we can do. I threw on a sweatshirt and shorts and padded down the staircase onto the tiled kitchen floor and picked up a book on the way to the couch. The green leather felt cool under me on a late Spring morning as I poured my heart out in words. I wrote down a few thoughts:

1) *Find a church*
2) *Find a pastor or counselor*
3) *Go on dates*
4) *Be the wife James wanted*

I looked through the closest churches to our new house we had bought in May of '99 and there were three Methodist churches within a short driving distance. One was in Cary, one in Algonquin, and one in Barrington. The first was 12-15 minutes north, the other 15 minutes west, and the last about 12 minutes east. Where should we start? I asked James about it once he finally got up, had his black coffee, and warmed up for the day. Again, part of our polar opposite ENFJ and ISTP personalities, means one is a morning person (me, usually by 6 am) and one is not (8-9 am for James). One of us wakes up before the alarm and cannot wait for our feet to hit the floor and the other mopes until caffeine surges through their veins and they feel alive. On the other hand, that means by 9:30 pm, I am not really good for much. But I digress.

This also means one of us likes facing conflict head on and the other does not. One of us likes pets, and one does not. One wants more kids than the other, one likes to live in the city and one on a farm, and yada yada yada. People have told us that we are so different, there really isn't much they can find about us that agrees. Except, there is that small fact that we met, were immediately attracted to each other's personalities and physical appearance, fell madly in love, and then fell equally out of "love". We were committed, we were always faithful, and we had strong resolve to make our marriage work, yet we did not possess the faintest idea as to how to fix what was broken. We tried talking and also giving space (which turned into days and weeks then he forgot what we were arguing about). We tried going on double dates at times just to have fun, laugh, play games, and then let ourselves banter. Those were fun nights with dear friends like Ryan and Elizabeth who we both adored.

"Going to church has got to be the answer," I reasoned with myself. When we met, I told him I knew Jesus and wanted to know if he did. I was fully aware that he had gone to church all 18 years until leaving for college yet didn't read the Bible, or do Bible study, or have Christian friends to advise him like I had. I drifted from those friends when I graduated college and moved three hours away from our university. Long-distance calling was expensive, we had virtually no money for plane tickets, and everyones' careers seemed to take us in different directions. I no longer stayed in touch with my high school youth pastor and his wife nor the youth group kids who were now in Minnesota, Florida and other parts of Chicagoland. Who could I talk to that would understand?

We decided to try multiple churches until we agreed on one that felt comfortable for us both. James grew up Methodist, so those are the only churches I suggested. I knew he would feel more at home and the service style would be familiar and undaunting. The first one we visited had a contemporary flair with a band with guitars and drums, and people sang, worshiped with their hands in the air, and I loved the music! I felt like this might be our new church home! James was uncomfortable with the demonstrative response from the congregation and this was not the place for him so we did not go back.

The next church was in Cary and in an affluent community not far from our home. The pastor was very intelligent, personable and engaging. His sermons were thought-provoking and drew our attention right away. James resonated with this masculine pastor who was polished and well-spoken. We sat close enough to one another on the hard dark walnut-colored wooden pew, yet as his custom, he never put his arm around me. I craved affection more than any other form of commitment. This had been true for many years. (I had extreme insecurity which did not allow him to relate to me the way he preferred, instead, I vilified him.) James had not been a touchy-feely guy since birth and nothing was changing him. I watched the couples all around the church and noticed those whose arms were draped around one another's shoulders, or men who reached to grasp their wives' hands during the service or while walking together. To say that I desperately longed for that was an understatement. What could I do to get James to love me that way?

The weeks turned into months and the senior pastor whom we both respected and admired took a position elsewhere. Neither of us liked his replacement as she was a solemn older woman with a different demeanor and none of the charm, passion or wit to which we had grown accustomed. Since we were not established in the church with friendships or the clergy, we slowly began staying home and withdrew from our Sunday worship.

Then something miraculous began to happen. I turned my focus towards my current life situation. I began to embrace my job in a brand new way, made some friends at work and began to find joy and gratitude in the little things. My Mom was consistently telling me, "Bloom where you're planted!" I wanted to have an attitude of gratitude for a multitude of things in my life.

So, instead of focusing on the failure that I felt in my heart about our marriage, I had a flickering hope that we would not only survive, but get over what felt like this gargantuan mountain of misunderstanding and emotional isolation that we were both experiencing. Always an avid exerciser, I would work out 6-8 times per week doing cardio workouts at Lifetime Fitness, went biking or lifting weights after work and on weekends, began Tae-Bo in front of the TV on cold winter nights, and began to work on myself. I read books voraciously for most of my life, beginning in elementary school, and rekindled that passion while I rode my exercise bike at the club, passing the hours engrossed in stories that immersed my thoughts in lives far more exciting than my own.

I climbed the corporate ladder at work, earned promotions, got very physically fit, and obsessed over my weight. In college, I had been on the scale 10 times each day, when I got up, every time I used the bathroom, before and after every meal, and after exercise. It was a mental cage in which I lived for decades, yet I had never put words to it or shared much with friends or family. In hindsight much later, I was able to admit that this was a form of an eating disorder by undereating and overexercising in order to maintain a "perfect" weight. Food had been my nemesis.

Although these were momentary distractions and goals upon which to put great levels of time and effort, the elephant in the room still remained. Our marriage was one of distance, disunity and division. We still did not see eye-to-eye and we were passing time, possibly both simultaneously hoping that time would bring healing where words could not.

Summer came and it was full of celebrations, time with friends in our home for Independence Day, an upcoming McKnight family vacation to Epcot in Florida, and time with my family in the backyard with BBQ's, yard darts, and more. We kept up the facade that we were okay as we engaged with our families and friends, trying to laugh and allow the daily blessings of enjoyment with others to keep our minds off the painful reality of how lonely we both felt. The weather was amazing that year, which meant more outdoor bike rides, backyard hangouts, games, and twilight conversations well after sundown with my folks. We played cards and large group games when my brother and his girlfriend gathered with us.

That July, my company hosted their 50th anniversary picnic in a gorgeous park with an outdoor pavilion on a perfect, warm, sunny and delightful Saturday. Hundreds of employees were eating, laughing, reminiscing about the early days in which our Jewish German founder had emigrated to the United States, obtained his green card, and began a legacy for the next 2 generations. His son had followed suit and was at the helm as CEO and was brilliant at his role. James and I made conversation with a large number of my co-workers, who I adored, and we laughed the day away. This felt so normal, I thought! How amazing. Maybe there are glimpses of a "new normal" on the horizon.

We left the party as the games and food were packed away from the lush green lawn, said good-bye to my work friends, and made the short drive home to pack for our family vacation to Florida in the morning. What would this next week look like hiding the state of our estrangement from his folks? Could we mask it? Would it be exposed, or would this vacation help us to heal? I would have my answer in the next ten days.

About 4 days later, after the 22 hour drive to Florida, time in the hot tub, playing tennis, going to Islands of Adventure, and sitting in the hotel apartment watching "My Dog Skip", I was happily exhausted. I wiped my tears from seeing the ending of this sweet movie about a boy and his best friend, a dog, who became his only companion day in and day out. Saying good night to James and his folks, I brushed my teeth, threw on my pajamas and found my side of our double bed in the dark. I laid down thinking about what a fun few days we had and another day at an Orlando theme park lay ahead for the next early morning. As I slept that night I had a very stark dream. Dreams of babies filled my mind. Actually, one baby. My baby. I envisioned having a baby and the baby was...a girl.

The next few days held games of shuffleboard, the amusement park, dinners out, and gorgeous sunsets near the hotel. A fitful night of sleep wondering about the state of how things would be between me and James when we got home, and the odd dream about having a baby left me in a state of curiosity. I went to sleep again with my mind racing with all sorts of thoughts and finally, alone in the dark hotel room, hearing conversation beyond the door in the apartment living room, I drifted off to sleep.

Overnight, the vague dream of nights earlier about being pregnant and then somehow "knowing" I was having a baby girl led to a second dream of having a baby again. In the dream, I saw her and I held her and the longer the dream continued I awoke with one stark detail. She had bright red hair.

I shook off the sleep from my eyes and around my face as I awoke this final morning before packing and making the long two-day drive home. The trip here was 22 hours and now it was pouring rain and that was all that was sustained in the foreseeable forecast. The thought of keeping this to myself, and not finding out if I was truly pregnant was plaguing me with curiosity. I had not dared tell James about it early in the week, not knowing what his response would have been, but a few days later I had found a silent moment alone to tell him about my dream, my intuition and how this was constantly on my mind. The second part of the trip, I had stopped using the hot tub and decided not to ride the fierce roller coasters that last day, avoiding telling our family the real reason for my apprehension.

"You will not mention this to my parents at all. You will wait until we get home to talk about this again," he answered gruffly.

My greatest fears had been realized as he had no desire to talk about this incredible blessing of the possibility of having a sweet baby, nor did he want to allow me to take a pregnancy test for almost six full days. The suspense was killing me. When was my last period? Surely, I would *know* immediately if I were pregnant, right? Don't women have this innate sense of just, well, *knowing*? A plethora of thoughts spiraled through my mind as we packed the suitcases, took trips down the three flights of stairs to the parking lot, and waved good-bye to the Florida sunshine. We were heading back to cooler and far less tropical Illinois. How was I going to sit for two whole days in the car and *not* talk about the one thing I was thinking about most? Wouldn't most husbands want to talk about the most exciting news his wife could have ever shared with him? Why wasn't he elated like I was? Of course things were not ideal between us, but wouldn't this cement our marriage in a brand new way, giving us joy and focus on our new family and growing closer for a healthier future? This seemed like a gift from Heaven. This was a glimmer of hope.

Miles and miles elapsed on the tires of our van as I voraciously read book after book those two days. We stopped for a few hours in Central Illinois to see James' extended family from North Carolina. His cousin and girlfriend were recently engaged and none of us had met her yet. I felt selfish wanting to just hop in our car as fast as possible and rush the additional two hours north to put my obsessive pregnancy thoughts to rest at last. We made small talk and I tried to remain calm and discuss random topics as we caught up on their lives in North Carolina. I kept giving that knowing look to James like,

"Can we please get going?" which he dismissively ignored, rightfully so as we seldom saw them.

At last, we hugged Mom and Dad good-bye, thanked them for a generous and fun vacation, and fired up the engine of the Mustang to head north. Those two hours felt like an eternity as I begged James to pass our home and go the extra mile and a half to Walgreens. I scanned the aisles for pregnancy tests and chose one with two tests in one, just in case. I had no idea what I was buying or what to look for, so this seemed like a good idea. The young 16-year old pimpled teenage male cashier looked down at the box, up at me and James, scanned our faces and quipped, "My parents had me and my Mom drank Mountain Dew when she was breast feeding me. Kept me up all night!"

A teenage boy is giving me breast feeding advice when I don't even have the slightest idea If I am pregnant, how to give birth, whether or not I will breastfeed, and what to eat and drink once I do. What on earth possessed him to blurt out this random story at a time like this?

"Uh, thanks, that sounds like a bad idea. This is all we are buying. Thanks," I replied, embarrassed. James handed him our credit card, and we asked for a receipt and walked speechlessly to the car.

We didn't talk on the short trip home, the stress and strain filling the car. I ran upstairs with the paper bag and box in my hand to our extremely overheated loft, having set the thermostat up high for the multiple days away. My mind was dizzy with thoughts as I tore off the cellophane, read the directions, prepared the washcloth and soap, and a clean, dry spot on the bathroom sink. I changed into clean, fresh-smelling clothing as I noticed now how I was sweating profusely as my heart pounded with anticipation.

Well, this is the moment of truth! In ten minutes or less, we would know what the next year of our lives held. I took the white and purple stick into the bathroom with me and allowed it to be saturated as required. Taking a piece of toilet paper and laying it on the sink, I rested the plastic applicator on the paper gently awaiting the results. I paced around our brown carpeted bedroom floor for minutes, seemingly wearing treads in the carpet. One minute, two minutes, three minutes, four minutes....should I wait longer to make sure it "takes"? Okay... I will wait five full minutes to be satisfied with the results.

James was nowhere near the bedroom during this time. He was seemingly painstakingly slow unloading all of the luggage from the car and loading the dirty clothes bags into the laundry room off our first floor kitchen.

What was taking him so long? Why is this so hard! I have been waiting a week already, why was he not up here to find out what is going on?

"James! Come up here, please!"

Waiting to hear his footsteps, I told him I was going to look at the results if he didn't come quickly. He emerged in the doorway after ascending the stairwell into the loft leading to our master bedroom. His stoic expression said it all, but I ignored his features, inviting him to walk towards the bathroom to look at the results with me at the same time.

My hands shaking, my voice quavering and desiring so much for the results to be positive, I picked up the box to review what I was looking for once more in a positive result. The indicator displayed two vertical lines inside the purple and white oval-shaped windows.

"Positive! It's positive! We're gonna have a baby!" I threw my arms around James' neck and gave him a big hug. The rest of the day was a blur in which I cannot remember a shred of detail. I don't recall his response, how he looked, what else was said, unpacking or making dinner, or planning for work the next day. I was simply stunned. Hadn't I been warned, however? I had multiple dreams, my period was a few days late when we left for vacation, and now I knew for sure! My lifelong dream to be a mother was going to come true. What kind of Mom would I be?

Chapter 13:   The Arrival

Philippians 4:4 - "Rejoice in the Lord always, again I say rejoice!"

The months cruised by going to obstetrician appointments, out to dinner to celebrate, lamaze classes, car seat installment training sessions, shopping for newborn furniture sets, and scanning through lists of baby names. As much as James and I disagreed on, we 100% agreed that we were not to find out the gender of our baby. We believed that God would give us his choice and we would love and raise this baby to the best of our abilities, no matter the gender or the baby's health. We would be grateful and celebrate this gift of life!

I was assured, however, she must be a girl after those dreams I had. First, I dreamed I was pregnant, then she was a girl, then a redhead, and now as the seventh month approached, I dreamed she would weigh 7 lbs. 6 ounces. I couldn't wait to meet her, kiss her, hug her and see her beautiful face! Only 3 more weeks, I thought, as I dressed myself for work in a maternity top and skirt for my corporate job that morning. I do not know how many more days of work I will actually have, so I need to keep my list of open purchase orders clean and on track, update my team in the Purchasing Department at the close

of business each day, and go home with a "baton handoff" ready to give to my

other Buyers if I have to head to the hospital. Those March days seemed to

drag by as I awaited this bundle of beauty and joy! Then, on a Tuesday

morning, I was walking to lunch grabbing my food when I began to feel sick.

My lymph nodes seemed puffy in my neck, and I felt my forehead feeling flush

and wondered if I was coming down with a fever. How could this be happening

now?

I made it through lunch and completed some of my work telling my

boss I was not well and needed to get home because of the baby. "Oh God,

please heal me and let me be right back to work so that my baby can be born

while I am healthy! She needs a strong Mama giving birth!"

The next 8 days I laid in bed with a fever, not taking any fever reducer

or any "medication". Our family grew up homeopathic and holistic, taking no

drugs of any sort, really only vitamins, minerals and supplements. I drank

fluids and slept in to gain immune functioning, I cross-critched for hours a

day, napped, read, watched bad daytime tv talk shows, and prayed for a healthy

delivery. Did I really believe strongly that God was hearing all my prayers

then? I do not recall. He wasn't my Daddy yet, He wasn't my best friend, I didn't know how incredible He was then, but I was clinging to hope that I would not go into labor while sick and pass illness onto our baby *and* perhaps keep others out of the delivery room. "God, I need this fever to break and soon!"

Finally, my fever broke and I returned to work mid-March. My co-workers had been great trying to cover my workload, but our manufacturing company was in prime season for sales and our eight buyers worked feverishly 7-9 hour days each day, five days a week making hundreds of calls, creating contracts, scheduling shipments, and meeting very harried and near-impossible customer deadlines. We built point of purchase displays for massive companies like Nike, Reebok, Rockport, Adidas, Sephora, Walgreens, Proctor and Gamble, Wal-Mart and more. Being the sole steel and aluminum buyer for our division, I had upwards of $2-$3 million in metal and residual purchases to make each year, and that meant hundreds of purchase orders, follow up calls on shortages, and scheduling my own freight to be delivered. When any of us were absent, picking up slack amongst the rest of us was quite challenging. We were all cut from the same cloth, however it seemed. Type A personalities with crazy multi-tasking abilities and a flair for adrenaline-rush work environment filled our cubicles. That is what I thrived on!

For the remainder of my third trimester before any contractions began, I knew I had to tie up as many loose ends as possible. One night, March 20th, 2002, I headed home after handing off my open orders list to my boss, and left like any other night. Our due date was originally April 3rd and had been moved to March 31st. I had expected to get up, go to work on that first day of Spring the next day, but the Lord had other plans.

Around midnight, I began feeling what I later found out were contractions. Between 1 am and 6 am, I laid in bed repeatedly obsessing over when to wake James and how long I could wait to call the doctor on call. For hours, I glanced intermittently at the green digital read-out on my nightstand clock which felt like hundreds of times, rolled over incessantly, trying to find a comfortable position, and then repeating without success. This went on for almost five full hours before I finally saw the clock click 5:55 am. I felt safe getting up, showering and brushing my teeth before calling the doctor as soon as the clock announced 6 am. Her office said when contractions are less than 10 minutes apart we were to grab our bags and hop in the car and rush to the hospital.

Ironically, on this March 21st morning, the official first day of Spring, snow fell all over Chicagoland. The trip that usually takes 7-11 minutes to drive to the hospital took over 40 minutes. I was asking James to put on music that would help me focus on Lamaze breathing so I wouldn't hyperventilate. Never having been through this before, I had no idea what kind of pain to expect. To me, this felt like pain levels of 5 or 6 out of 10, although seasoned mothers might disagree. I was wishing now I had eaten a meal sometime between 1 and 7 am before we hopped into the car. I had forgotten the horror stories of 24 to 48 hour labors with *no* food or water! What was I thinking? Oh, well. Here we are in rush hour traffic, plodding through heavy spring snow, ironically, making little headway as our baby might choose to make an appearance into the world before the car arrives at the red Emergency Room doors.

"Please don't let my water break before we get there," I prayed. Not only would it be an embarrassing mess in the car, but I had no idea what James would say if this all happened while he was trying to focus on driving. Fortunately, my Dad was still living about an hour away (before moving to Florida, permanently), so we began calling our family members one by one to let them know we were headed to Good Shepherd in Barrington. James' folks had a two hour drive on dry roads (longer in these winter conditions) and they packed up quickly and rushed north. My Mom and stepfather lived two towns west and planned to come after breakfast, and James' brother must have taken off work that Thursday afternoon so he could drive up with his folks. The waiting room grew fuller as the hours of labor wore on. One hour, two, three, four, five, six.....no food, no water, no water breaking, and very little dilation or signs of full labor. This little one was certain about when he or she would be arriving and had a set plan, or so it seemed.

Being sedentary on my part, yet wishing for a faster delivery, we sought suggestions from the doctor. After eight long hours, she suggested the possibility of breaking my water to move the process along much more expeditiously. Finally, closer to dinner time (in which I was not eating, of course), she came to offer to break my water bag and get contractions moving more vigorously. This meant my pain level skyrocketing, unfortunately. Thus, the next two plus hours were a blur of activities. I was laying completely flat, sweating more than I can recall with all my cross country and track races combined, with a few cool washcloths to my forehead, and I had James' hand to hold and squeeze. The bright overhead lights of the birthing room ceiling glared down on my writhing body. The pain was so intense at times that I felt tunnel vision setting in that usually preceded me passing out or fainting. This had never happened while lying horizontally before, so the instance scared me at the thought of losing consciousness while doing the most important thing I had ever set out to accomplish.

The waves of dizziness and fainting passed with the news that I was now dilated to 10 cm and effaced, which meant the baby can safely enter the birth canal and less damage will be done to me in the process. The epidural took partial effect after one hour and the left half of my body was somewhat numb and the right half mostly numb. It was like someone took a magic marker and drew a line of symmetry down my body from my neck to my torso and half of me had almost no sensation and the other half was screaming with an overload of sensation. I practiced the lamaze breathing, but it was challenging, to say the least. James was doing a stellar job coaching me on breath pacing and remembering to put my visual focus far across the room as breathing was my main task at hand. Holding my breath to exert additional force on the baby continually for seconds on end took most of the reserves I had after 22 hours with no food and only 4-5 hours of furtive sleep. I was afraid of what everyone might be seeing watching this delivery, as I had never had anyone see me uncovered like this other than my Mom as a young girl and I was overly modest since I hit puberty. The thought of strangers, especially men, coming into the birthing room was a bit terrifying, however, the only concern on my radar was bringing this sweet bundle into the world

healthy, breathing, and through natural means. I did not want surgery at any

cost. That had been my 9-month long prayer. No episiotomy, no C-sections.

"Please, God, hear my prayers."

The angry Russian nurse was back in the birthing room asking me

questions, and I was not a fan. She asked what my pain level was with a

graphic set of faces on a spectrum from smiling to balling tears, 1-10, and I let

her know I was probably an "8".

She admonished, "No, you are more like 5!" in her curt, harsh Russian

accent. Are you kidding, lady? Why on earth did you ask if you already knew

the answer? Can I please have a nice nurse who might hold my hand, say

something sweet and encourage me as a total novice? I had Helga the Hittite

telling me I wasn't in pain. I pushed her brusque words out of my mind,

momentarily, as the doctor came back to check on how much progress had

been made over the first hour of pushing. Since the process was taking so

long, my ob/gyn, Dr. Lamond, was also seeing other patients on the maternity

floor while popping in and out checking on the progress of Baby McKnight.

Active delivery began around 5:15 pm. Finally, closer to 7:30 pm, the

doctor asked if I would be willing for her to cut an incision to make the baby's head easier to emerge from the birth canal. We had learned about this during our birthing classes and were told extended recovery time was necessary to fully heal following this procedure. An episiotomy had not been my first option, but I was weary after all the straining and wondered how much energy I had left to muster.

"Okay, if that is necessary, yes," I replied discouraged.

"This should allow the next few pushes to be more productive," Dr. Lamond explained.

So, within minutes, I was numbed, doctor's scalpel in hand, and poor James who had to find other places to look around the room, sat with me until it was over and the next push was required. This was the moment of truth we had been long awaiting since that Walgreens trip in mid-July to buy our first pregnancy test.

Waiting for the signal, I breathed slowly in and out and conserved as much energy as possible. Hopefully, adrenaline would be my friend and I would be victorious on the next few attempts. "Okay, watching the monitor for this next wave, the contraction will work in tandem with you to push the baby's head lower and out. Here we go.....push!"

I must have grimaced, gritted, and held my breath and pushed for dear life, literally. About 5-7 more, and the baby was crowning with beautiful long wet locks of hair. The doctor gave us a little play-by-play and some encouraging news with each one. Fortunately, she wasn't ducking out to head to other rooms anymore, she was committed to us and our baby, so I needed to give every effort humanly possible.

At 7:48 pm on the dot, a gorgeous bundle of joy entered the world on March 21st, 2002 in Room 320 at Good Shepherd Hospital in Barrington, IL. James and I looked at each other and waited...."It's a girl!" Our faces broke out in massive smiles, the tension and apprehensive waiting in the rearview mirror, as we fixed our eyes on the most beautiful baby we had collectively ever seen. "Hello, Lilly Mae, we are your Mom and Dad!" The next several minutes raced by as Apgar scores were measured, an umbilical cord severed, azithromycin put into the baby's eyes, nurses cleaning up the fluids from the area, the doctor delivering the placenta, and all other post birth procedures. This was so new to us and as people rushed in and around us completing their duties and recording on charts, they pulled in a cold, metal harsh scale and set our brand new daughter into it fairly nude. She began to cry with the cold touch to her skin and someone announced, "7 pounds 8 ounces!"

"Wow, she was so much smaller than I expected! Imagine if she had weighed more like James and his brother at birth, or their cousin who was over 10 pounds! I guess I got off easy with her delivery," I conceded. I sighed relief and exhaled slowly knowing that she was safe. Our prayers were answered.

The nurse asked to take her down the hall to wash her up and bring her back in to breastfeed. At first, fear gripped me at the thought of her not coming back. What if someone took her, how could we get her back, what recourse do we have? Surely, they take extra special precautions. The nurse put a matching plastic bracelet on Lilly that matched mine. It bore her name, date, parents' names, room number, and all of the vital statistics. The barcodes were scanned and matched to ensure mothers and babies were properly reunited and all would be well. As promised, about 20 minutes later, which honestly seemed like an eternity after months of waiting for this wee one, the nurse carried her into the room, all cleaned up, bathed, hair washed, and a pink knitted stocking cap on her large noggen.

"She has red hair!" we both exclaimed. Just like my dream. Coincidence? I didn't think so.

Her head looked so big compared to her tiny shoulders with her stocking cap removed and body swaddled tightly in the hospital blanket.

James began inviting our parents into the room, the Grandmothers were first. No news about the baby's gender, name, or vitals were shared in the fleeting moments he dashed into the waiting room. My dad had long since gone home, as this was a 12-hour labor after all, and several of the family members had arrived before lunch. Now, well after 8:30 pm, he made the long drive back to the city and would come visit soon. The grandmothers crept into the room, opening the door slowly, and as soon as the pink cap was seen from the doorway, they both burst into tears of joy.

"It IS a girl!" they beamed. This was a delightful celebration as Lilly Mae became the first official grandchild on both sides of our family, each of us with a sole younger brother who were both bachelors in their early 20's. Lilly Mae would surely be the talk of both grandmothers for months and years to come as she would take center stage.

My Mom and James' Mom took turns holding her and cooing over her while James was delivered his "hero" meal post delivery. The dads apparently got steak, potatoes and sides with a drink of their choice. The kitchen had long since closed, so they didn't have anything for me, so I believe they brought an apple and small snack. Since I hadn't eaten in so long, I needed to eat a little bit at a time until I could stomach an entire meal as the medications wore off. I was ravenous. Watching James eat that steak was very hard at the moment! Alas, I had the beautiful gift of a sweet baby to love and nurse and love....and it was only just the beginning.

Overnight, sleep was fleeting as I heard the rustlings in her clear plastic bassinet all night long. She would need to nurse again soon. Would I be able to figure out how to position her in the dark and with so much fatigue in my brain? What was a football hold, and could I get her into position properly with all of these blankets and pillows?

Long about 2 am, I was trying desperately to get Lilly to stay under my right arm, lay on the pillow at just the right angle, open her mouth at just the right time, and make sure she formed a proper seal. Oh my, this is not for the faint of heart. There are so many things to remember! Would this get any easier over time?

I began almost crying when Lilly was clearly ravenous and I tried to nestle her in just the right way to satisfy her need for food when she just kept crying and turning her head side to side. "We have to work together, little one!" Out of frustration, I pressed the call button. When I heard the voice from the other end, I blurted, "I need help with my daughter!" Daughter, oh my, yes, I have a daughter! That sounded foreign and like a dream all in one word. I am a Mom! Finally, after 20 years of imagining, planning names and wishing and hoping, this is really true! I have a living, breathing gorgeous daughter.

The sound of the nurse entering the room startled me, momentarily. The nurse explained that wrapping her in the perfect swaddle was key. Lilly looked like a Baby Burrito. Next, she helped me put one more pillow under my right arm, positioned her head higher than her feet in the football hold, and got her to turn her head at just the right moment to begin nursing. All of the muscles in my body must have let out a unanimous sigh of relief as I felt my heartbeat begin to return to normal, my thoughts slow, and the sound and sensation of my daughter receiving her second meal of her life brought tears of gratitude to my eyes. I settled in, leaned back, and let my body rest.

Celebrating the homecoming of sweet Lilly Mae was memorable and nostalgic. We dressed her in a white Winnie the Pooh outfit with snaps up and down the legs, a matching hat, buckled her securely into her carseat, checked the straps to infinity, and carried her to our car. I rode in the backseat with her, ensuring her floppy infant neck didn't cause her to stop breathing while James crawled home below the speed limit. The trip home on dry pavement was not 40 minutes like in the snow, but we were not setting any land speed records, either. As we parked the new VW Passat in the driveway, we unclipped the carrier from the car seat base, James grabbed the bags and Lilly, I had my diaper bag, and we walked carefully up the sloped pavement towards our porch. I remember walking across the threshold and making this place our new "family home" as we cried for joy at the celebration of our baby girl and all that life had in store for us as a family of three.

My sleep-deprived brain and overtaxed body did not wear well over the first many weeks with a newborn nursing every 2 hours like clockwork. Lilly seemed to have an oral fixation, drinking over 30 minutes per session. That meant only 90 minutes maximum between feedings for me to sleep, eat, shower, get dressed, or be human. I liked to say in those days that I was a "juice bar on demand". Out of desperation, we appealed to friends on how to survive this initial phase and train our girl to be awake during the daytime hours and sleep at night. A friend recommended a book which I devoured in less than 2 days and implemented the same day I bought it. We subscribed to the theory of "Babywise" which trained the baby to eat, play, sleep, repeat. This cycle allowed me closer to 2 ½ hours between feedings to recover. This was the only way we made it through, I think. The cycle was predictable and we were doing our best to play with her, enjoy time with her, snuggle, take pictures and get her to eat before she cried so much she swallowed too much air.

The days were full and long yet so rewarding. I journaled almost an hour per day about all things "Lilly" and the newness of Motherhood. The evenings were hard and somewhat lonely once James returned to work. He commuted 44 miles to work, completed a full 9-hour day, then made the long drive back home. I certainly missed people, interactions, conversations, going places, and feeling like a viable adult. A few calls to friends and co-workers broke up the long 12 hour days alone with Lilly, and I talked to her all day long about everything. Cameras on the walls of my home might have shown people I was crazy for how much minutiae of life I explained to a one-month old baby. I told Lilly everything! This kept me sane, also demonstrated my naturally loquacious way, and I felt less alone as I interacted with her. Little did I know that our worlds were about to get rocked.

Chapter 14 : Home Improvements

Philippians 4:19 - "God will supply all of my needs according to the riches of His Glory in Christ Jesus Our Lord."

A few Saturdays after Lilly began sleeping 3-4 hours at night and before the final weekend of maternity leave, James promised to repaint the garage door and spruce up the front of our home. After all, Father's Day weekend was coming up soon and we were hosting both families due to the birth of Lilly. Everyone would be driving to see us this year for the first time. James headed out mid-morning with a long list of painting supplies and drove to Home Depot one town north of our house. He is known for taking an hour or more to scour the shelves for the best deals and being deliberate about getting everything needed on the first trip so there are no wasted trips. A half-hour turned into 45 minutes, into an hour (granted the store was a 15 minute drive from home), and then extended past that. I knew this might take awhile since getting paint mixed to the perfect hue required bringing paint samples from home, using the spectrophotometer at the store, and test runs to match it just perfectly.

While home all morning alone with Lilly, I tried the same usual "tried and true" soothing techniques to get her to be calm, rest, and take a nap. She was fussier than usual and just simply irritable. I attempted to use the vibrating bouncy seat, checked her diaper, burped her, rocked her, walked her around the living room, and then tried the back porch on a sunny June morning. Nothing was working. She wasn't hungry, gassy, wet, or anything I could discern.

"What is wrong, sweetheart? I kept asking her, which was of course, a rhetorical question for a 12-week old infant. "What else should I do?" We were outside on the deck, with Lilly in the shade on her vibrating bouncy chair. She began to fuss again, so I gathered her and her blankets up and brought her toys inside, resolving to call my Mom for some grandmotherly wisdom. I bet she will know something else I can try.

I layed Lilly on the red, black and white Gymini mat with criss-crossed fabric poles that had a cute octopus toy hanging down from one of its grommets. Mr. Octopus hung just the right distance from her face to incentivize her to reach up, use her eyesight to focus on him, and swing her arms up to touch it. This was a perfect training mat for babies to help their vision and dexterity.

I grabbed our white cordless phone from the base and walked over near the mat, plopping down criss-cross applesauce on the carpet a few feet from Lilly as she laid on her back, playing happily. Dialing my Mom, I thought, how should I phrase this? What advice would she give me?

"Hi, Sweetie," my Mom answered, seeing the caller ID.

"Hi, Mom, I called to talk about Lilly since she hasn't calmed down all morning and is incredibly fussy. There's something wrong, but I've tried everything and I am scratching my brain trying to figure out what else I can possibly do to get her to finally fall asleep."

Just then, I heard a foreign sound, a staccato metronome-like repetition that I could not distinguish nor had I ever heard before in almost 30 years on earth. My peripheral vision picked up an odd rhythmic motion created by her limbs, and I said, "I think she's having a seizure, I have to go!"

I hung up the phone, scooped Lilly up off the mat, raced to the front door, and ran to the neighbor's house to the north of us. With James gone, I was all alone, and I needed to get Lilly help ASAP. Hitting the doorbell, I prayed that the 40-year old married couple were home. Mrs. Woodbury answered immediately, and she saw we were in distress and asked, "Cassie, what's wrong?"

"Lilly is having a seizure, her eyes just rolled back and her arms and legs are jerking. James is in Crystal Lake so I brought her over here."

"Did you call 9-1-1?"

"Not yet," I replied, as she picked up her phone and immediately dialed the emergency hotline.

"Yes, this is an emergency, we have a baby having a seizure...young, yes, less than 3 months old. Yes, come as fast as you can!"

She continued giving the address and closest cross-streets as well as the nature of the emergency as they promised to get an ambulance over as soon as traffic would allow.

Walking into their home, I assessed Lilly's features closely and saw a blue-hue forming around her lips as her eyes were still rolled back into her head. What did we learn in middle school Health class about seizures? Turn the person on their side, right? (I remembered when a classmate, Leslie, fell out of her chair, passed out and had a seizure in class during junior high school.) I dropped to my knees and laid her on their front hallway rug to turn her on her right side. She appeared to be done seizing and her breathing returning to normal. Her sleep was long overdue, yet this was absolutely not the way I anticipated she would enter into it. What was taking James so long and where was the ambulance? I was in a panic.

A few moments later, I looked down to recognize I was still wearing my two-piece swimsuit as Lilly and I sat on the back deck enjoying a gorgeous June spring day in the sunshine before all of this unfolded. Barefoot and ill-prepared to rush off in the ambulance, I couldn't have cared less about myself or my condition as the only thing my mind could obsess about was Lilly's health and current unresponsiveness.

Moments later, the wailing ambulance sirens filled our block on Glacier Parkway as the white emergency vehicle came into view. I thanked the neighbors, and jumped into the ambulance with my daughter. "Tell us what happened to your daughter," the first technician commanded.

I told my story to the EMT's as the driver navigated traffic towards Sherman Hospital in Elgin. I would these critical details numerous times later at the hospital in the ER, to the doctors, and on and on ad nauseum throughout the day. No medical personnel seemed to share any details that I divulged with each other. Why couldn't they just write this down and share notes so I didn't have to hash through the same questions every 10 minutes? Can't someone please simply help my Lilly?

Meanwhile, Mrs. Woodbury had called James and he dropped everything in the shopping cart and sped down Algonquin Road to Route 25 and south to the hospital. Ironically, my Mom heard the wailing alarm of the ambulance pass her house about 12 minutes after I abruptly hung up our call and she said, "My granddaughter is in that ambulance!" I don't know how she knew, but she was certain of it. Grandmotherly intuition, I guess. She and Ned took off in their car and headed south to the hospital knowing which way the siren was traveling. No calls, no cell phones, just sheer instinct and intuition. They beat James to the hospital by a few minutes and were able to join me and Lilly in the ER waiting room.

"She's postictal and might be asleep for awhile," the attending physician informed us.

"What do you mean, what is that?" I asked ignorantly. I had no idea what these medical terms meant that they were using.

"This means that your daughter's body went through a lot during the seizure, which is like an electrical storm in the brain, and her system is resetting by sleeping until she can regain strength and homeostasis. She should sleep for an hour or two. She should be fine. Seizures are common, especially in babies. Did she have a fever?"

"No, why do people keep asking that? I have explained 6-7 times to each person who has asked, she has been sleep-deprived for months since she was born, she has a hard time falling asleep and staying asleep and today she was fussier than usual. She ate, played, I did everything I usually do to care for her or calm and soothe her, and she would not take her morning nap. I called my Mom to ask for help when all of a sudden she started seizing."

"How did you know it was a seizure, ma'am?" asked the clueless intern.

"I have seen seizures on TV and a girl had one in my classroom back in junior high, and I just knew. Her arms and legs were moving together at the same time and I remember learning about tonic-clonic seizures. I think that's what Lilly had. That's all I know," I said defensively. (In retrospect, I believe they were ruling out abuse and ensuring DCFS did not need to be called. At that moment, the thought of them accusing me of harming my own baby never once entered my mind.)

"I will have some additional questions for you, ma'am, however, it doesn't appear we can help her here as effectively as a hospital with a NICU, so we are authorizing a transport for her to St. Alexius Medical Center in Hoffman Estates."

"We're leaving? When? I don't understand, why didn't the ambulance take her somewhere where she can be helped? Why are we wasting time if no one here can help her?" I asked, incredulously.

James jumped in at the right time interjecting, "Sweetheart, I know you are upset, but this man is just doing his job. Sir, can you please explain what you have tried to do for our daughter here and why she needs to be transported? Should she move in this condition or is it best that she regain consciousness first?" James was always so patient and reasonable even under pressure. He looked caringly at me and placed his hand on my bare shoulder while he spoke to the nurse.

"We have run bloodwork and checked her vitals, but she really needs an EEG, which is a neurological test that will allow pediatric doctors to understand the origin of the seizure in her brain and discern the root cause, if possible. The NICU will take great care of her and they have pediatric neurologists on staff who will do an excellent job for your daughter. We refer people there all the time. I am sorry for your frustration. The ambulance would not have been allowed to make a 20-mile transport for an infant in distress. It is completely against protocol," the doctor calmly explained.

"Thank you for your explanation, I understand, " I said dejectedly. I was incredibly scared and angry, simultaneously.

The nursing ER staff had been working with others getting them loaded for another transport, doing intake, and running tests in and out of the Emergency Room. One sweet nurse saw my plight wearing my navy blue and white two-piece swimsuit in a cold air-conditioned Emergency Room and brought me a green oversized medical scrub top to at least cover a portion of me. Being half-dressed, hungry, thirsty, and now tired myself from the stress of the day, I still didn't really care about the plight of my own situation as I focused all of my attention and energy on Lilly. Certainly, it was embarrassing, but my usually socially anxious self thought very little of my situation. My attention was on Lilly and my fears about her future were only just beginning.

"We're ready to take you girls, now," added the EMT who entered our curtained room to share the good news.

"Okay, James. Well, we'll see you at St. Alexius. Please call your family and let them know where we are. I'm so sorry that you cannot come in the ambulance with us, I wish you were with us," I conceded.

"I know, but I need to bring our car, so it works out...I'll be right behind you, don't worry!" He smiled a wan smile and watched us go.

I smiled a weak smile in return, glanced away as I walked next to the gurney rolling Lilly towards the exit doors into the parking lot. This is so surreal. I was supposed to return to work in a few short days when my 12 weeks maternity leave expired. How can I ever leave my baby now? But work was the absolute furthest thing from my mind.

Chapter 15:   Angels and Miracles

Hebrews 13:2 - "Do not neglect to show hospitality to strangers, for thereby some have entertained angels unawares."

NICU nurses are "angels" with skin on. Period. (Not Heavenly angels, of course, but they serve like they are gifts from God, for sure.) These fearless women made my four, sleepless, fear-filled nights survivable in the NICU with Lilly. I was in fear, had swirling catastrophic thoughts, I was barely eating and showering, and simply staying near Lilly's bedside watching over her. I was fretting far too much. We conversed with visitors as they came to see our little family in the tiny glass-enclosed NICU room. The grandparents came and stayed for hours, sat for long stretches awaiting the neurologist's updates, and pined away the days. Our daughter was on prayer lists at tiny nearby neighborhood churches, the megachurch, Willow Creek, and on the lips of those we had never met and never would. We were humbled by the cards that came from strangers over the next few weeks saying they were praying. I was dumbfounded. Why would strangers pray for a little girl they never met? I had not met people like this before and it astounded me at their kindness. I will never forget how that changed my perspective and outlook on what authentic

Christians must really be like. I had no idea what intercession was then or how important prayer is to the heart of Our Heavenly Father.

I had longed to go to church as a little girl and only went in the two years I lived with my grandmother as she raised me in an urban town where we walked every week to Catholic church. She taught me to pray the rosary, and I fell asleep almost every night clutching the beads, fiercely, almost like the power of my grip determined the answers to my prayers. Prayers that my Mom would come back to be with me. Prayers that my Dad and his new wife would accept me and prayers that my new step sisters would invite me into their lives. But that was a lifetime ago now. I had been in church dozens of Sundays in my high school years and into college. At my university, I had no car to drive myself to church and very few churches sent shuttles to the college students to pick them up. Tragically, my church attendance came to a stand still during college. After graduation, I went with James to restore our marriage, and then once the pastor left the church, so had we. What did I believe? Did I believe the Bible was true, that Jesus is the Son of God and died to take away my sins? Yes, I believe He is the Son of God, the Savior of the world, I believe in Heaven and Hell, and in angels and demons. But did I know Him? I was soon to find out just how little I knew about His character.

Towards the end of our stay in the NICU, Lilly was scheduled for an MRI to rule out tumors or anything in her brain causing the seizures. James and I agreed that we did not want any invasive procedures and we certainly didn't want her given drugs and chemicals to harm her vulnerable little body. We were told that if she did not fall asleep to go into the tube for the MRI, she would have to be sedated. We both were adamantly against that. Lilly never sleeps deeply during the day, and she almost *never* falls asleep without vibrations, rocking, walking, music, or some stimuli. This is just the worst case scenario, I thought.

As James' parents came and sat in the room with us, we gave our consent to the neurologist on staff, and they were planning to wheel her down to the lowest floor in the hospital where the MRI machine was stationed. We just sat proverbially holding our breaths until they came to take her gurney and locked in the guardrails in anticipation of the trek down the long sterile corridors. Lilly had just begun to doze off a few minutes before, and they prepped the tubes and fluids attaching them for transport. Within 15 minutes, we had descended many flights via elevator and were walking down the long dim vacant basement corridor. I kept hoping she would sleep on her own. (Or was I actually *praying* she would sleep?) Lilly needs to stay asleep because we can't give her those drugs! What will happen to her if they have to sedate her at only 3 months old? I held my breath and waited.

The X-ray technicians got the room ready, put the coverings over Lilly and strapped her into this contraption that made her look like she was in a baby casket. It was quite grotesque the thought of her in a literal box, velcroed in place across her legs and chest knowing that the sounds from the MRI machine would be incredibly loud and disturbing for anyone, let alone an innocent and unknowing infant. The great news was that her test would last under 20 minutes due to her small size, and her sleep cycles are closer to 40 minutes. We were pushing our luck, and time was down to the wire.

The technicians offered James and I lead aprons and instructions if we stood in the room with Lilly. He opted to remain behind the glass during the test, and I donned the lead apron and pushed into the exam room. Wild horses were not keeping me away from my only daughter! Beginning a dull whir, the machine began to spin louder and louder until the sounds set my teeth on edge. I kept crying as I stood in the back right corner of the room watching the technicians moving dials and inputting data as the test progressed. The only movement seen throughout the entire ordeal was Lilly's tiny pacifier swiftly moving up and down as she habitually sucked in her sleep.

It was actually a precious sight. I will always remember, because it reminded me she was not in a coffin, she was still alive, and this would all be over soon. I hoped. Once and awhile I would turn looking over my left shoulder at James through the glass. I was wishing I could hold his hand during this ordeal. At last, the sounds died down, the whirring stopped and the platform Lily lay on retracted out of the tunnel. Now, we will await the results.

We took the long walk back down cavernous hallways, into the elevator, ascended back up to the NICU, and walked until we found her room and my in-laws there awaiting the news. The nurse wheeled the gurney back into position and began reconnecting the wires and IV fluid to the metal stand when my father-in-law cracked open a cold can of Diet Caffeine-Free Coke. Lilly shot up like a rocket with this minor sound. She had slept through the long trip both ways, the prepping, strapping, clamorously loud knocking sounds from the MRI machine and a tiny two-cent piece of aluminum caused her to wake up? James and I rapidly turned to look at one another in unison with incredulous looks on our faces. Then, at a knowing glance, our eyes agreed, there was no way on earth that was an accident. We just witnessed a miracle. Amen!

The four long days and nights in the NICU at St. Alexius yielded new information that Lilly most likely had no genetic cause to her seizures, that they were not life-threatening, she does not have a metabolic disorder, nor a brain tumor, and they have absolutely zero understanding of the root cause. Those days changed me, my focus, and birthed new fears for the plight of my daughter. I was brought to a deeper place of desperation than I had reached in all my three decades of trials and suffering.

As James and I made the quiet drive home after being discharged, I again sat in the backseat watching Lilly's every breath as I had on the drive home from her birth. Different hospitals, different fears, same beloved daughter, and same loyal James. Her future seemed to hang in the balance and the devious creeping machinations of my overactive brain wore me down. The weight of these burdens at times were suffocating. Would she ever be able to swim in a pool if she had a seizure disorder? Drive a car? Go to prom? Would she be labeled "epileptic" and be on medication for the rest of her life? Would anyone want to marry her and care for her if she couldn't drive? The thoughts plowed forward for months overwhelming me with foreboding questions about her now very uncertain future.

Sleeping on Lilly's bedroom floor became near impossible as I slept a miniscule 30 minutes at a stretch night after night, as my return to work date fastly approached. What if our licensed babysitter we agreed to pay would not take a "special needs" baby? What if Lilly had a seizure while in her care? I was sleep-starved and barely remembered what day it was. I would say good-bye to James in the early hours before 7:00 am so he could drive the long 44-mile commute to a Western suburb to his reliable corporate job. We needed this job and its benefits as well as the tremendous income it provided us. All I wanted to do was quit my job and stay with Lilly. James was adamant I stayed at work. "Our daughter will grow up to know she can be anything she puts her mind to! You have a great mind, and you are using it," he stated with persuasion.

I was crushed beyond crushed. How much money did we need? When was enough really enough? We weren't yuppies, we didn't need new cars or fancy vacations. We had a wonderful home that was perfect for us and a growing family, very low mortgage and we carried no debt for anything except our house. We bought used cars that were certified and in excellent condition. I cut hundreds of coupons and went without new clothing (I hate shopping, fortunately), pricey groceries, beverages at restaurants, and cut every possible corner to save as much money as humanly possible. In fact, besides the obsession of getting on the scale almost a half-dozen or more times per day my other obsession was being as frugal as possible with all means necessary. I scrimped, saved, sewed holes in clothing, wore out the elastic in my clothes over a dozen or more years, and still wore my things from high school and college. I even reused my plastic sandwich bags when packing my peanut butter and jelly sandwiches. In hindsight, the level of this fear of not having "enough" is really quite astounding. The magnitude of these obsessions drove me to make decisions and sacrifice hundreds of activities, opportunities, times with friends, family and coworkers. In retrospect, I forsook most of my teen and young adult years frantically trying to save more and spend less. I am sure I offended people, unintentionally during these decades, and sadly, risked relationships and my reputation because I was such a miser. Watching "A Christmas Carol", I am sure I related to Ebenezeer Scrooge on several levels, yet I did have a heart to help people. I had no idea how to enjoy spending money on myself or casually using it for fun or "frivolity". Still, all I wanted to do was quit my job and be a stay-at-home Mom.

Thoughts like these and others filled my mind as I desperately tried to cling to a few hours of sleep each night on Lilly's rough carpet near her crib.

Out of desperation, I realized that neither my will power, my accolades, my body being a perfect size or my ability as an athlete, nor graduating with highest honors from High School or college could save my daughter. None of my personal efforts and accomplishments could save Lilly. I could only pray. Finally, in sheer exhaustion and desperation laying on her bedroom floor, I cried out to God. "God, I can't do this anymore. I am barely functioning. I need sleep and I need your help. I have to sleep in my bed....If Lilly needs me, I need you to wake me up." Little did I know at the moment, He heard every word, and would fully answer in a bold way eighteen months later.

Chapter 16:   Beauty from Ashes

Isaiah 61:3 - "Provide for those who grieve in Zion, to bestow on them a crown of beauty instead of ashes, the oil of joy instead of mourning, and a garment of praise instead of a spirit of heaviness."

The first year after these scary hospital visits began to fade as we went into treatment mode, ensuring she had her phenobarbital multiple times per day mixed with a tablespoon of breastmilk, counting the months between seizures, and following the neurologist's protocol. Life went on as usual with me at work full-time, James now owning and running his own fledgling energy company out of our home, and Lilly at daycare a few blocks down the street with Miss Linda. Miss Linda was another unasked answer to prayer as she loved the kids in her care like her own and did not turn Lilly down due to her seizure disorder. She watched a little boy with Down's Syndrome, Eli, and twins in which the male twin had cerebral palsy, Grant. She watched several children and ran a tight ship offering healthy meals for each one. She kept vigilant nap times from 9:00-11:00 am and 1:00-3:00 pm for the babies. Lilly flourished under her care. I never wanted to be a full-time working Mom, however, I was embracing the positives in every stage we faced. James' rookie business could not support our family as he earned a scarce few thousand dollars for the first annual year after inception. My corporate salary and benefits paid for Lilly's neurological care and her two prescriptions. I was making some friends at work who were Christians and becoming cherished confidants. My Mom was always telling me to "Bloom where I am planted" and I tried to grasp the attitude of gratitude in various hardships. We couldn't go out to dinner on our current budget nor enjoy a vacation, but we had Lilly, our home, our health, our families and so much more. We were abundantly blessed. I would have a glass half-full mentality for the rest of my life, and that is a true gift from God.

Lilly was a delightful baby as far as her insatiable curiosity and her personality. She also innately created a unifying effect on our marriage which was obvious to both me and James. We did not go through any explicit healing or confront and resolve the extremely distant years, but we kept plodding forward. Our mighty family of three seemed to have the motto, "I think I can, I think I can," as chanted in the classic children's tale. We were the "Little Engine that Could", alright. There were some serious mountains on the horizon that we could not even yet faintly distinguish.

To rewind several months, the first mountain absolutely blindsided us. One day, James was in an extremely high corporate position in his energy company in which they truly relied on his expertise, savvy knack for understanding all things in the energy trading market, and his wisdom in making deals. The owners of the company threw a big shindig at the COO's house in a very affluent golf club community. James and I got dressed up, attended the party with paid caterers dressed in tuxedos, hors d'oeuvres galore, and all the alcohol you could consume. Fortunately, I didn't drink and James had cut way back by this point in our marriage. However, people always act like morons when they drink too much and there were rumors and gossip flying at this party. None of which, however, betrayed what was about to happen at Dixon Energy Incorporated.

The next month, an audit was called, corporately, in light of the federal Enron scandal that had recently rocked the nation. Thousands of employees were without jobs and the energy industry was flooded with applicants and a minimal amount of openings across the USA. The same auditors who were contracted to evaluate the accounting and business practices of Enron also audited Dixon. This meant, a careful scrubbing and analysis of the financial dealings. All of the profits and losses, the bottom line, accounts payable and receivable were painstakingly reviewed with a fine-toothed comb. At the end of this period, the top four corporate employees, including the party-throwing COO were arrested and brought up on white

175

collar crime charges of embezzlement. This left the company completely bankrupt after greedily adulterating the receivables which falsely inflated the earnings by $4 Million. When the paper shredders were searched as well as digital files, and employees subpoenaed and questioned, the true P & L margin for the company was over a $1 M loss. The phony customers and fraudulent invoices were created to erroneously demonstrate a gain in the black so that the top tier managers could take their five-figure bonuses and head to Aspen on posh ski trips. The lower level employees like James and his department were now faced with a company in bankruptcy. Would all 100 employees lose their jobs because of four greedy men with no conscience? Time would tell.

Over the next four months, James was paid hefty retention bonuses to remain each subsequent month. At the end of every 30-day period, the liquidation company would cut James McKnight a $10,000 bonus and thank him for his loyalty and dedication. As a young family, we had counted on his salary to pay off car loans, our mortgage ahead of schedule, and sock away nearly $20,000 of savings that would afford us a cushion for our children's college fund. Additionally, we planned to have a second baby and cover my loss of income during maternity leave. During these four months, some of James' closest co-workers approached him about starting a brand new energy company that could compete with Dixon when it was running on all cylinders. The current Purchasing Manager, Accounting Manager and Sales Director had a well-balanced skill set but they needed an account guy who was brilliant with numbers, sourcing, and legal contracts. James was their first-choice for their fourth and final business partner. The men met on weekends and stayed up talking by phone until late after Lilly and I went to bed. We even met their wives and children at backyard gatherings during the planning phase. While I didn't feel like I fit in with these much more fashionable and polished corporate wives with school aged children and ten years on me, I felt like we had a promising new chapter just around the corner.

James accepted the first, second and third retention bonuses which paid all of our debts, mortgage, loans, and caught us up on any medical bills remaining from Lilly's birth and two hospital stays for her seizure condition. During these 90 days, he was staying up as late as 1:00 am on weeknights combing through the contract language and legalese his new partners required for this start-up business. Viator Energy was slated to launch in just another month as all three partners were severed from Dixon in advance of James due to the nature of their roles as well as their over-inflated salaries. James was an ideal candidate to retain on many levels and he would help do "clean-up" of the financial shambles Dixon found themselves in. The Viator "owners" graciously allowed James to work evenings and weekends (and a great deal of time away from me and Lilly, I might add) during these months while he wore a multitude of hats. He had less and less time to be a husband, new daddy, son, brother or friend.

As the trip to Springfield was imminent to legally incorporate Viator in the state of Illinois, James was abruptly abolished from the ownership of the company. No explanation was given, no apologies that justified the betrayal, just the simple decision that they couldn't wait anymore for him to be full-time with them and legally separated from Dixon Energy. This was the harshest, most painful rejection of James' life. He had many disappointments on sports teams he adored as a young boy and teen, rejection from girls he had strong feelings for, and even severed friendships which caused extreme anguish. Having hopes and dreams of providing for his family and working shoulder-to-shoulder with three friends was a dream come true that he had never dared to dream. It felt like a gift on a silver platter at the initial invitation.

Presently, staring at the stark reality that Viator would open their offices and begin selling energy with a fourth man who was enlisted to replace

James McKnight was like a dagger to his heart. James is an incredibly loyal person, friend, family man and co-worker. He has integrity, is kind, courteous and caring. He does not even hang up on nagging telemarketers. What had James ever done to deserve something like this?

The first months and then year after this betrayal was a constant wound that would keep reopening as James worked 40-hour weeks with no income attempting to birth his own energy business. This went on for over 9 months. Finally, a man in town cut him a break and began paying him $2.00 for every data entry he made for his business. Late into the night, outside our master bedroom door, in the loft at the top of our staircase, the click, click, click of James' computer keyboard indicated his relentless pursuit of providing for his family.

More mountains came in unexpected ways. James' two closest, beloved men in his life were contacted by Viator since they had industry or sales experience. Soon, these two beloved, trusted, and loyal loved ones were enticed by the promise of dividends and sales structures with benefits to boot. This was highly attractive to these men who needed medical benefits, had no college degrees to their names, yet had sales skills to spare. They were well-trained in cold calling, pounding the pavement, driving long miles to make sales calls, and whether Viator deliberately set out to crush the wounded and bruised soul of James McKnight or not, these men said "yes" to the job.

As James' wife, this was the hardest season of our marriage aside from the strain between the two of us. James grew up in a close-knit farm town community in which your word was as good as "oak" and a hand shake meant a promise. James' fierce loyalty to everyone he loved and trusted had always been sincere and authentic. This reality of his heart being crushed again in such short proximity to the first betrayal put me over the top. I lacked wisdom in how to best support, love and encourage him to heal through this. Without the Lord at this time, we did not know to pray, weep at the Lord's feet, and we did not have a support base of friends who worshiped Jesus to point us to the healing that only He brings.

At that time, we did not live by Jesus' tenacious command to forgive or invite the Holy Spirit to make this possible. We would have experienced a very different level of freedom during hardship and trials. We both know in retrospect, as the Lord promises in His word to bring "beauty out of ashes" (Isaiah 61:3) and to "make all things work together for the good of those who love Him and are called according to His purposes" (Romans 8:28), that these traumatic events were just what wooed James to the cross in the first place.

Chapter 17   The Final Mountain

Psalm 121: 1-2 "I look my eyes up to the hills. Where does my help come from? My help comes from the LORD, the maker of Heaven and Earth."

Before every valley, there is a mountaintop experience. We cannot descend into the valley without having been at a higher elevation preceding this moment. In order to give Glory to God yet save a lengthy explanation of events, I will be succinct. After many emotional and convicting discussions about our financial situation and whether or not to grow our family, this decision boiled down to what is best for our family and ultimately for our children as forever friends. I reasoned with James that as an "only" child myself and with his brother being five years younger, having the benefit of siblings close in age would prove invaluable. (Praise the Lord, our children are extremely close as adults!) I told him that God would provide for us if we chose to have another baby in these difficult financial times. Somehow, deep down, we both knew that trying to have a baby was the right choice and if it was God's plan, He would bring about the baby we were longing for. We both yearned for a son to join Lilly and to have just two children, due to our dual-income household, it didn't seem viable to spend more than $300 per week on childcare and James was still adamant about me working full-time.

A friend shared a fertility book about planning conception to more likely determine the child's gender. For months, we set out to plan the conception of a baby brother for Little Lilly. After reading the book and following all of the steps, painstakingly, waking up at 5:15 am even on weekends for four months in a row to chart my temperature, I kept a running tally of fertile days and the right time to conceive a boy. In January of 2004, after four false negative pregnancy tests and one false negative blood test, six weeks later, we found out that we would be having a sweet addition to our family around the first week of October that year. Lilly would be just 2 ½ years old, potty trained (I hoped) and ready to meet her "brother".

While watching the NBC primetime fall sitcom launch that fall on a September night, I couldn't finish my dinner due to feelings of indigestion and pressure I couldn't quite describe. Having been through this once, the symptoms were completely different, nonetheless, we went to the hospital in a matter of minutes since my Dad was eating dinner with us when this all unfolded. He was in from Florida for a few months and would stay with Lilly until James got back. Arriving at the hospital around 7 pm that warm

Thursday evening, Marcus William McKnight was born at 1:33 am in a quiet delivery room with just us, "Far From Home" playing on the corner TV for three hours awaiting dilation, and one doctor and one nurse. This was such a juxtaposition to Lilly's daytime labor in which there was a steady stream of hospital workers in and out of the room that whole day long. With little fanfare, and a very peaceful birth after 3 strong pushes, his peach fuzz blond head popped into sight and soon we were holding him! It was the baby boy we dreamed of for years, rounding out our family, perfectly. We were beyond blessed. During four months of early morning wake-up calls to chart my underarm temperature, all had been worth it. This tiny investment into the rest of our lives as the McKnight Family culminated in this Jubilee moment. We were elated.

The exuberance of having a baby, celebrating his birth, hosting visitors, having Lilly come in her sundress and hospital visitor sticker to come kiss and hold her baby brother were priceless. This was the best kind of bliss on earth. The dynamics in our family were emerging. The gift of loving this sweet newborn bundle of joy and nursing him just melted my heart.

Chapter 18   Dichotomy

Lamentations 3:22 - The steadfast love of the LORD never ceases, his mercies never come to an end, they are new every morning, great is your faithfulness."

Around 1974, Daisy's world was experiencing an ironic dichotomy. On one hand, her marriage was falling apart. On the other, she had prayed and waited nine years to become a mother. This was her greatest desire and goal since she was a little girl. She yearned to have a baby girl of her own to love, cherish, and nurture in a far better way than she was ever cared for by her broken and neglectful parents. Now that she and Harold had finally conceived and carried a baby to full term, given birth to her, and Daisy could be a stay-at-home Mom, her ultimate dream came true. How was her marriage completely falling apart?

Harold was no longer the center of attention in their home and Daisy was now spending all of her time, energy, thoughts and devotion on baby Cassandra. Daisy was in ecstasy to know that her days were full of wonder, delight and mystery unfolding in her adventure of being a fledgling mother. Any sleepless nights or difficulties with newborn crying was easily replaced with the joy she felt holding her sweet girl. At last, she could fulfill her life's calling of being a mother. Daisy read books, talked to other mothers in the park, chatted with women by the neighborhood swimming pool, and took long stroller walks in the afternoons along the narrow cement sidewalks of the condominium complex. She felt so alive. All day, she would talk to Cassandra and explain what the birds were doing, how the sky looked, the formation of the clouds, why the sun was going down in the sky, and explained every nuance of life to her ad nauseum. Daisy's curiosity and fascination with the beauty all around her came alive once again as she began to see it through her daughter's innocent and unknowing eyes. The journey to becoming an invigorated and satisfied woman was unfolding for her in the most spectacular way.

The days turned to weeks as Daisy and Baby Cassie enjoyed sunshine, gardening in the cool of the morning, walks, naps, afternoons at the pool, and evenings in the kitchen making dinners before Harold returned from work. One particular evening, Daisy rushed Cassie home from the pool to bathe her in the master bathtub. Afterwards, she swept her own shoulder-length red hair up into a plastic comb and donned her favorite apron. Beginning to saute a medley of vegetables for their dinner, Cassie began to cry, unrelentingly. Wondering what could be upsetting her daughter to such a strong degree, she held her, soothed her, and swayed her slender hips side-to-side standing in their narrow rust-colored kitchen trying to bring her some solace. Minutes elapsed and Cassie would not settle or come into a place of peace, despite Daisy's best efforts. The telltale key rattled in the lock from the echoing hallway and the bronze knob turned left as Harold swung the door inward. Daisy tensed up at the thought of Harold's negative mood darkening the bright day she had enjoyed with her newborn baby. This caused Cassie to cry with more determination.

"Why is that baby always crying when I come home?" barked Harold, accusingly.

Daisy defended her by saying, "She is just so delightful all day and we have the most incredible time together and sometimes she just gets fussy. It's not her fault."

Placing Cassandra into the frontal cloth baby carrier, she cinched her up more snuggly than usual, and went about preparing the vegetables and rice. Proficient in the kitchen as always, Daisy had a culinary feast assembled in record time despite her crying daughter, plates on the table with matching placemats, and neat cutlery at each place. She filled two glasses with fresh ice water and summoned Harold to the table for supper.

As he sat down to join her, she placed a now docile baby into her carrier on the kitchen floor where she could watch her parents enjoy their meal together, quietly.

"How was your day?"

"There's not much to tell. The guys at the bank can be a real piece of work you know. Same ole, same ole. What did you girls do today?"

"Oh, we had so much fun! We watched the cardinals and the robins taking off from the grass beyond the railing early this morning from the back porch, then picked some mint from the garden, and went on a walk with Barb and Matt from upstairs. The weather is just pristine in early July mornings so we get out early to feel the breeze as we walk. She is simply the best neighbor to have with us both having newborns together and becoming mothers for the first time, we have so much to talk about and…" Daisy trailed off at Harold's uninterested and far-off look as he chewed his food.

"Sorry, I don't mean to spoil your dinner with so much chatter, it's just that I love being with Cassie all day but I need more conversation. It's just not the same as having adults around. You know."

"I don't have any idea, really, but glad you have the neighbors. That's great. Can you make my broccoli so I can cut it with my fork next time? It's really hard to chew," Harold complained.

"Yes, sure, sorry, I know you don't like it al dente like I do, I'll simmer it longer next time." Stunned at his inability to converse with her yet finding a way to insult her cooking once again, she paused to decide what to say next. "What are your plans for the evening?"

"Read the paper, then listen to that series I just ordered through the mail, that Philosophy course I am taking, and head to bed by 10:00. Then, up again early to head to the office for the closings that are scheduled tomorrow."

"Okay, do you mind if Cassie and I play in the living room tonight?"

"Yes, actually I do, I want to spread out all my books and have my legal pad to take notes and the bedroom is too small to do anything in there, really. Can you play somewhere else?"

"I suppose we can. I can......I'll think of something," she said, contemplatively, as she carried the empty plates to the sink to wash.

"Where did all of this go so wrong? How did we get to this cold emotionless place of feeling like roommates in the same home, light years apart, my serving him and catering to his needs like a mother instead of a wife? Did he appreciate me at all? Was he realizing that I wanted to talk to him, spend time with him? How could he only care about himself, the present moment, and not think about me or his only child?"

Daisy's mind swam with questioning confusion. The answers could not come as rapid-fire as her questions were being sent out. Daisy did not have the grounding of seeking Jesus for answers nor the Holy Spirit for comfort nor God the Father for His perfect embrace that fit every occasion. She stood there barefoot on her olive green linoleum floor feeling lonelier than she had in a long time and knew this could not be all that marriage was intended to be.

Over the next two years, she grew in confidence as a mom and taught Cassie absolutely everything she knew that could be absorbed by a toddler. Ultimately, she realized it was time after all of the harsh words, mental anguish, cold-shoulder and selfish demands that she would ask Harold for a divorce. This was not decided simply. A lot weighed into this decision. Twenty long years of being belittled in front of family and company had reached a climactic moment. He mocked her frugal habits, insulted her looks (although most would label her beautiful by worldly standards with her Hollywood figure, auburn hair and all), and caused

division when visiting her family for holidays and other gatherings. She

never wanted to admit failure to her mother or anyone else for that matter,

but her baby girl did not deserve to be in this environment with an unloving

and selfish father who didn't know how to love either one of them. She had

no idea how she could find a job that would support their needs and live

alone, but she was sure like heck gonna try.

The Methodist church a few miles away hosted a Montessori school

inside, Monday through Friday. Looking into the classes, tuition and

curriculum, Daisy was impressed. This was far less costly than daycare and

Cassandra would be learning to read, tie her shoes, and participate in music

classes. Also, the school would offer socialization with other children,

teach math and art and Cassie would be fed healthy meals each day around

noon. Naps were in the afternoon where they slept in their own individual

playpens and the workers seemed so caring and gentle with the children.

What a Godsend! This was the best solution, as it was ripping Daisy's heart

out to go to work and leave Cassie in the hands of anyone else, let alone

strangers. Now all she needed was a full-time job with benefits that paid a

decent wage for women.

Looking through the want ads in the local suburban newspaper, there were a plethora of secretarial jobs in the late 1970's. Women were called upon for many jobs that men would never stoop to take. After attending community college for two years, Daisy had mastered the art of typing over 100 words per minute with one typographical error and was a whiz at both stenography and shorthand. These were all impeccable job skills that would help her land a stable job. After determining where to look, she decided upon Numeridex Incorporated, only 3 miles down the street from her condominium. Her interview was a success and Daisy was offered the position at a modest $7,500.00 annual salary. It was only a fraction of what Harold earned and provided for their family of three, but it would have to do. Daisy's middle name was "frugal", so she would make ends meet, as always. After all, isn't that what her childhood upbringing had taught her in spades? "Waste not, want not!" she heard her Grandmother's voice echoing through the recesses of her memory.

Asking Harold for the divorce was harder than she thought and he blamed her for all of their failings and shortcomings. He could not even begin to fathom why she would leave a handsome, well-spoken lawyer like him to be a single mother who would be simply scraping by. Daisy knew that without this dark cloud hanging over their household each day that she and her daughter would have a home that was full of kindness, joy, and love the way she always foresaw it would be.

Around three months later, Harold finally moved into his mother's house near Chicago and said his good-byes to Cassie. Calling her into the living room on that long, uneven rust-colored shag carpeting, he sat down on the olive green hassock and looked Cassie in the eyes. "Daddy has to leave, honey. I am moving out. I won't be here every day, but I will still see you."

Cassie's three-year old brain began spinning with lies from satan about how it was her fault her parents had a wedge between them, her fault that their marriage failed, and now she felt abandoned by the only father she had ever known, as distant and emotionally removed as he was. He was, after all, her Dad.

She began to cry, not knowing what all of this meant. And how could she possibly? Her mind was so innocent, unknowing and pure, she did not know about unforgiveness, silent treatments, or emotional abuse. She only knew the rose-colored world that Daisy painted for her day after day where they found insects inside and carefully protected life by taking them outdoors. Daisy taught her to play games without any vengeful tactics (Daisy would not allow them), and look to the good in all people.

After saying good-bye to her father that day, darkness entered Cassie's heart on that cool Autumn afternoon, and it would take up residence for decades to come.

Chapter 19   Marcus' Miracle

Psalm 150:6 - "Let everything that has breath Praise the Lord."

Life continued for the McKnights with hills and valleys including the

demands of a family with two young toddlers. Marcus had just celebrated his

1st birthday on September 17th, in which our family, friends, and Lilly's

preschool buddies came together to celebrate. The event possessed much less

fanfare than when Lilly turned 1-year-old which is common in second born

children.

Now, two weeks later, I invited James to his first Christian rock concert

praying that he would choose to trust Jesus as His Lord and Savior. We

attended Petra's 30th anniversary farewell tour as James prayed the sinner's

prayer in a whisper next to me that night. I was so full of hope that evening as

we made the long trip downstate to pick up the kids at Mom and Dad

McKnight's home in Central Illinois. I slept soundly as he drove late into the

night not knowing what the next few days had in store for us as a family.

Only the Lord knew that our son, Marcus William, would be fighting

for his life on October 5th, 2005. That evening, James and I jumped into our silver VW Passat, buckled him into his carseat, and I drove erratically through the same twists and turns to Good Shepherd Hospital. Ironically, this was the same anticipatory route James had driven the morning of Lilly's birth, 30 months earlier. The drive was familiar, however the circumstances were quite foreign to us both. We were holding our breaths in fear for his life, not knowing why he was respirating more than once per second with shallow, ineffective breaths. Marcus was such a happy-go-lucky baby, and nothing seemed to rattle him. The fact that he was wheezing, out of sorts, and lethargic were huge red flags to the baby sitter hours earlier. Her urgent call to James alerted him that Marcus must be picked up, immediately. I was a 30-minute drive away at a corrugated manufacturing company taking a tour with my Supply Chain Manager when I got the call. Making my apologies brief, I took off in my high heels clacking all the way through their cement floored warehouse out to the gravel parking lot and my awaiting car. Racing home, I purchased a vaporizer at the closest Wal-Mart, also running through the cold tiles of the store as my heels made a loud clickety-clack sound of a frantic mom trying to help her baby boy.

Arriving home around the same time, James had held him and gotten him settled into a nap, which seemed to be the best thing for his exhausted little body. Filling the new vaporizer with water and some Vicks Vaporub, I set it near his crib, praying he would begin to have some relief from his respiratory problems.

When he awoke violently from his nap, he was wailing away with real tears streaming down his tiny overly pink baby cheeks. With the sun setting now, James and I knew we had to get him help as soon as physically possible and doctor's offices would all be closed. Not being willing to take the risk of the EMT's choosing the hospital we were taken to like when Lilly had her seizure, I insisted that we get into the car and leave right away. Calling my folks who lived 3 miles down the street, my Mom immediately went to her car grabbing her purse and keys as she ran out the back door into the garage. Those eight minutes seemed like an eternity as her large headlights finally came into view a half-mile down the straight street on which we lived. Lilly was on the back steps of the garage as James and I walked to our idling car in the driveway awaiting Grandma Daisy's arrival. We kissed her good-bye saying, "Grandma is coming right now...stay on the steps, we need to take Marcus to the hospital, Honey!" Unfortunately, this crisis scarred Lilly's 2-year old mind as fear set in with feeling abandoned in those few scant seconds. To us, it was probably 15-25 seconds, but to her tiny mind, her parents left her, and chose to help her brother instead.

Arriving safely at the ER, I threw the car into park, and James dropped me with Marcus' car seat carrier at the large revolving door as he ran around to the driver's side and hurriedly parked the car. Soon after, he met us at the intake desk. We rattled off statistics, dates, insurance information, symptoms and waited impatiently for Marcus' name to be called. We were seen very quickly probably due to the fact that the ER was slow coupled with the nature of his health crisis. The demeanor of the staff assisting us was pleasant as they silently acknowledged we were extremely worried young parents. This was just another Thursday night in the ER for them, and they were just as calm as could be.

As the nurse did an intake of vitals on Marcus, his little 12-month old body was writhing trying to catch a breath of air. He was breathing around 72 times per minute. The additional effort forcing in and out air, and breathing so shallowly helped to explain his lethargy, she explained. They ordered an immediate chest X-ray to get a grasp of what they were dealing with.

The next thing that happened was so unexpected. As we sat late into the night awaiting test results, Larry, the church usher who served with James at the 8 am Sunday service walked into our bay wearing purple scrubs. "Larry! What are you doing here?" I asked, incredulously.

"Well that's funny, I volunteer here every week for several years now, but never on Thursday nights. Someone switched with me which means I am here!" Coincidence, Lord? No way! I think you sent him here for us, especially for James. This is amazing. What is going on? A familiar and friendly face to bless James with a welcome distraction during one of the scariest nights of his adult life was a tremendous gift. Only You, Lord.

The men chatted, made small talk, and James filled Larry in on Marcus' seemingly mysterious condition. Multiple X-rays later, an ordeal with eight attempts to draw Marcus' blood from his dehydrated infant body, and another hour awaiting blood work results, Larry had long since left. They denied me the right to nurse my own baby and Marcus dehydrated more and more as the hours elapsed. "If you cannot get a blood draw on this next attempt, we are taking him to another hospital who can help our son!" I yelled, lacking compassion at this point in the wee hours of the morning.

Sleep deprived, scared, hungry, thirsty, and irritable by this point, I hit my breaking point. No more Mrs. Nice Mama Bear. If you are going to prick my son's little sweet body 6 times causing him to bleed and you have inept employees who shouldn't be working on infants, we are blowing this popsicle stand. I was absolutely serious. What were they thinking? Who in this hospital is trained to work with infants? What about the pediatric wing? The labor and delivery nurses? Isn't there anyone who can help us, Lord?

"You cannot take him out of the ER without being on an IV, ma'am. It is against hospital procedure," the nurse retorted.

"If you are incapable of putting an IV into him, then you are leaving us with no choice. Our son's life is at stake and we aren't going to sit and watch you dehydrate him to death when I can nurse him right now. I cannot believe this is happening," I complained.

"We have someone coming down from the 8th floor now. She's a phlebotomist. We are hopeful she will be successful on the first try."

"I am not sitting by and watching our son being poked and prodded and bleeding like this anymore," I insisted, resiliently.

Over the course of this time of waiting and this bloody ordeal, a police officer wandered down the ER corridors. He was looking for children to donate Beanie Babies to, ironically. He had been on duty and was on his last delivery. He peeked into our bay and saw James and I sitting on either side of Marcus' little metal bed rails. In his hands, was a pristinely white bear with white and silver wings. It was an angel. "Ma'am, I have one last stuffed animal to give away, and I wondered if your son might like it."

"Oh, yes! Thank you." I swallowed slowly, realizing the gravity of this gift from the officer at a time like this. He handed me the angel bear and I studied it carefully, reading his Beanie Baby Ty red-heart-shaped tag attached from the factory. I read his birthdate, his name, and the poem that accompanied it. His name was "Hope".

"Lord, did you send this man to deliver this sign of hope to us tonight?" I could not help but believe all of these "coincidences" were beginning to add up to quite a God story that we could not conceptualize in the midst of crisis. Larry being on call as a candy striper volunteer, the timing of my Mom being able to come stay with Lilly, the angel bear named "Hope" at such a time like this, what else, Lord? I was about to find out.

Quietly, as Marcus slept shirtless in his tiny white diaper, the glucose drip hanging from the metal portable stand near Marcus' bedside gave him life-giving nutrients. He desperately needed sleep, hydration and sugar to bring him back into homeostasis after all of the traumatic events of the night. Finally, peace at last, or so we thought.

After three x-rays , twenty-five phone calls to suburban and inner city Chicago hospitals, not one of them said yes to taking Marcus' case. The doctor said that he needed two critical things, a neonatal intensive care bed and an on-call surgeon to perform an emergency bronchoscopy. Finally, after hours of calling, Rush St. Luke's Presbyterian Hospital in downtown Chicago accepted his case. They had one bed left and a male surgeon who could fit him in late morning. Looking at the clock, it ticked a moment past 2:15 am.

The ground crew arrived around 3:30 am, after the 50 mile drive from Chicago to the Northwestern suburb of Barrington, IL where we eagerly awaited the news that would come next. I was exhausted. My face was tear-streaked and James hadn't had a wink of sleep either. We were beside ourselves with worry for our sweet son. James dropped to his knees at one point crying out, "We need someone to help our son!" in the midst of Marcus' bleeding during attempts to get him a glucose drip. The night had been full of raw emotion yet the Lord kept speaking to me and keeping me calmer than I had been in thirty years on this Earth.

Usually, I was prone to hysterics and overreacting at every possible obstacle in my life. Now, the Lord kept bringing back to mind an important point Daisy was reiterating and shared with me in a book she purchased.

"Power in Praise" was a gift she bought the previous Christmas which I finally read over the summer. During difficult times, we are to say, "God, I praise you." We can say, "I don't know what is happening or why, but I am praising you, Lord." Recently, a famous Christian band, Casting Crowns, released a song called "Praise you in this Storm" which had the repetitive theme that no matter what the circumstances, we will Praise Him!

Walking to the bathroom before 3 am, I desperately looked into the mirror. I observed my sleepless, wrinkled and aged face, and said quietly..."I praise You. I am choking out these words as I see my son in this condition, but I praise You!"

Over these next few hours, there was quite a lot of frenetic commotion. Our family had endured an almost 8-hour overnight hospital stay which required phone calls to our parents asking them to watch Lilly. Suddenly, our sweet son began involuntarily coughing. His vitals crashed and oxygen levels were dangerously low as his skin became mottled and took on a purplish hue. The quiet bay within the Emergency Room that had simply held myself and Marcus soon transformed into a live-action ER episode. Attending physicians, doctors, nurses, techs, and volunteers all jammed into this small trauma unit as the curtains whipped open from every side. Machines were blaring, monitors beeping, and Marcus's oxygen levels continued to crash. The purple-gloved nurses hovered around him and wanted to look to see what was causing his vitals to plummet. The nebulizer treatments that had been administered through his nose for hours, held by my determined hand, were suddenly removed and they began working on sparing his life. One final coughing fit changed everything.

The clear oxygen mask that enveloped Marcus's nose and mouth made all the difference that morning due to its transparency. After his last forceful cough, something ejected onto his tongue. "There is something on his tongue !" I exclaimed to the nurse closest to us. She rolled him onto his side, and taking her purple gloved finger swiped a piece of food from out of his mouth. As we examined it, we realized not only this was a huge piece, almost ¼" or more in width, also there were no signs of digestion, and it appeared to be a piece of ham. We suddenly exchanged shocked glances.

"Ham? When did we feed him ham?" We racked our brains to remember when we offered him meat to eat at his young age. It was now Friday in the middle of the night and it had been days since we had a meal like that with our family.

"We fed him ham at your Mom's birthday party at the buffet last Sunday after church! That was more than five days ago!" I informed James.

The doctor interjected to clarify what felt bewildering and puzzling at the moment. "Aspiration happens as food is inhaled into the lung instead of progressing down the esophagus into the stomach to complete digestion. Your son is very fortunate. Kids choke to death aspirating all the time. You hear warnings about hot dogs, balloons, popcorn and many things that can be accidentally inhaled and prohibit the airway from maintaining proper respiration. Your son is lucky to be alive," explained the ER attending physician.

Realizing now that it had been in his lung all week causing the breathing impediment, soon secretions of what could become pneumonia would begin setting in. The ER attending physician, Dr. Horcher, came closer to see what finally occurred with Marcus' coughing fit. His words will never dissipate from mine and my husband's memories.

He pronounced, "There is no doubt in my mind that God did not reach down and pull the meat out of that kid's lung. Infants do not have the capacity to cough food out of their lungs. It's not possible. I've been doing this for 25 years, and I have 4 kids at home. I would have been praying like you were. I saw your faith tonight." (I wrote a thank you letter to Dr. Kevin Horcher after that night.)

What seemed to be a random breathing situation, could have easily ended in a choking fatality right there in the ER. The ambulance ground crew we had waited many hours for was dismissed, and the flight for life crew was called in to helicopter Marcus to Rush Presbyterian St. Luke's hospital in Chicago. We impatiently waited another hour or more for them to arrive in which time Marcus' breathing and heart rate slowed and his oxygen levels increased. It was a miracle.

The helicopter pilot and his assistant nurse were incredible! They had 15 children between them and were so incredibly loving and compassionate to me and my husband the entire process of strapping Marcus to this little gurney that looked like a coffin, and rolled him off into the pitch black night sky. In the hours it took for the flight for life rescue crew to prepare the oxygen and additional nurse and ready the equipment in the helicopter, finally the sun began to rise over Good Shepherd Hospital in Barrington. The morning rays started to dawn as the chopper blades began to whir.

I hugged James good-bye letting him know I would land before he could navigate 50 miles of Chicago traffic in the Friday 6 am rush hour. I waved and walked towards the pilot and crew and just then, the news no mother wanted to hear came from the pilot's own lips.

"I'm so sorry, there is a nurse required to administer oxygen to your son during the flight due to the coughing incident he had. If he were to repeat that in flight, we would have to intubate him. The nurse is required to monitor him non-stop, and that means there is no room for you in the helicopter."

His words sunk into my chest like a lead balloon. My heart was broken and shattered in that moment knowing that for 10 grueling hours of fear and uncertainty, I asked the Lord for strength and comfort to make it through this difficult ordeal. I had praised Him all night long, at times, choking out the words.

When things looked the bleakest next to Marcus' mottled and bare chest, I whispered, "Is he going to die?" "Lord, why is this happening to our son? Is he going to die?" I had felt a whisper in my soul that said, "Today is not his day."

However, this seemed too much to bear. The hardest circumstance to stomach was to now stand with my husband in the grassy field near the helipad and watch our baby boy fly off into the red-streaked sky with complete strangers. What if they crashed and we never saw him again? How could I just watch him leave and trust them with our precious son? Just as I was about to

break down really crying, I asked silently, "God, why can't I go in the

helicopter? Why?"

His answer came suddenly and without pause. "Your husband needs

you in the car with him." And just like that, I had my answer. I was at full and

total acceptance. We would drive together, I would pray, James would drive,

and we would trust that Marcus was in good hands. He would drive while I

corralled family support to the hospital and ensured Lilly was taken care of

another day while the surgical team completed the bronchoscopy.

In retrospect, James and I both knew beyond a shadow of a doubt that

the Lord meant to keep Marcus here on earth with us for very important

purposes. One of those purposes was to bring my husband to salvation

afterwards. Additionally, He has grown my heart and gratitude, faith, and

ability to understand joy in the midst of trial. He has replaced my stubborn

pride and taught me contentment. We have no pictures from that weekend as

a camera was the last thing on our minds as we dashed to the car and raced to

the hospital that fall evening. The mental images are enough to sustain us and

reveal God's great character. He definitively saved our son's life. We serve a

powerful and mighty God.

About thirty minutes later, our son arrived safely for his surgery, and James' family members were already there to welcome the flight crew. Marcus' gurney was being wheeled into the hospital off the helipad. Knowing that Mom and Dad McKnight were there when he landed gave my Mama's heart so much solace in the moment. We sat and stared at red taillights all down the highway as we inched our way into the bustling streets of Chicago around 7:30 am. The drive took us over one hour longer than the chopper flight lasted.

The surgeon was prepped and ready to go a short time after we arrived, and I even asked for the "Hope" angel Beanie Baby to ride down the hallway on Marcus' gurney into the operating room. They agreed, even though they probably removed it before they scrubbed in for the surgery. They gladly appeased me and I watched the little bear riding high upon the white blankets near Marcus' side as they wheeled him through the double doors. I am sure I burst into tears as he disappeared from sight. The night had been long and wearying.

The bronchoscopy was quick and successful and Marcus was released later that weekend after giving him Augmentin to prevent a bacterial infection in his lungs and respiratory system. (In essence, they treated him for pneumonia). A few short days later he was his happy, cheerful infant self with a ravenous appetite. The pediatricians warned us that he would have lung conditions or asthma possibly for the rest of his life. I knew the Lord had other plans. (Marcus has gone on to be an avid three-sport athlete for years and now plays collegiate soccer. The Lord did not let that crisis divert his path at all! Praise Our Heavenly Father our Awesome Healer!)

We are abundantly blessed to be the recipients of his steadfast love and constant miracles. First, he saved Lilly, then he saved me as I cried out to Him for help with her condition, now He saved Marcus. Surely, James was next.

Chapter 20:   A New Family

Genesis 2:24– "That is why a man leaves his father and mother and is united to his wife, and they become one flesh."

Daisy and Ned settled into married life soon after the wedding in January of 1984 yet blending two households with completely different habits, schedules, eating styles, and disciplinary manners was easier said than done. It took hundreds of conversations, consulting a well-trained and loving counselor each week, reading books and hosting "family meetings" to begin working out the kinks of four fractured souls all living now under one roof. Corey determined not to call Daisy "Mom" and I the same with Ned, and reserved the name "Dad" only for Harold, even though he wasn't contributing in that role very much at the time. There were squabbles, selfishness, jealousy, anger and all of the common themes that run through creating a blended family. I didn't like sharing my Mom with Ned and Corey didn't like sharing his Dad with Daisy. Hard truth. It just is. Now what do we do about it? Two kids under the age of ten have no conception of how to not have tunnel vision and think about "me, me me". So, it was left up to the adults to work out ways of communication, spending time with us together as much as possible, creating new family traditions and habits that felt comfortable to all of us.

We began playing board games and card games on weekends, going for bicycle rides in the park in town, having family dinners absolutely every night (no exceptions) and the list went on. Daisy wanted to create the most unified and close family within her power. Her dream was to have us not only seem close but to truly be close. But how would that be accomplished? A lot of trial and error, a lot of tears, and a lot of hard, down and dirty "family meetings". Sigh.

Knowing that growing as a family and starting new traditions was important, they saved to buy a townhome in a better part of town that would send us to a more well-revered elementary school. So, saving and scrimping that first year, they were able to leave the tiny 2-bedroom, 1-bathroom apartment and move into a 3-bedroom, 3-level townhome with a tiny backyard, a carport, and an end unit with grassy space to run and play on the side. This became a utopia for me and Corey as we made friends in our new neighborhood. We played games every day after school and all day on weekends, like capture the flag, tag, stuck in the mud, and hide-and-go-seek games which were all the rage. We have the most vivid and fond memories of those ten years living in a place Daisy affectionately referred to as "Kidsville".

There were multiple parks, the swimming pool was just down our street

towards the main drag, plenty of miles of roads to ride our bikes with friends,

skitch on skateboards (shh...don't tell our parents), tennis courts where I

played a hundred hours of tennis through elementary and middle school, and

our neighborhood school 1 mile down through the squiggly streets of our

subdivision. I never knew that life could seem so....safe. The neighborhood

with teeming streets of jovial kids on every driveway, a plethora of antics to

find ourselves in, dogs to pet and people to meet was my dream come true.

After being an only child for almost nine full years, and playing solitaire until

my eyeballs bled and talking aloud to my stuffed animals, I was ready for

adventure.

On summer days, we would be up early, finish a few simple chores

that Daisy had listed out for us, then play all day with the neighbors. We would

swim at the pool, ride our bikes to our friends' houses for ice-cold Kool Aid

(Daisy had a no sugar policy so we had none of this ever in our house!) and

eat forbidden "junk food" snacks. We would cajole the non-athletic kids in our

neighborhood to still play the "tag" game with us we invented or capture the

flag, knowing they would probably still be too slow and get caught, but it would be fun, nonetheless. Our friends, Bryan and Barry, had a way of convincing anyone of anything. They were probably like two characters of the Little Rascals Gang, always looking for fun, but knowing unless others were involved, it would just be a boring summer day alone. They had a knack like Tom Sawyer getting people to "whitewash" the fence and convince them to get involved in shenanigans they would not choose to if not for their charm. They were the life of the party. The boys were always coming up with more inventive ways to play "Pig", "Horse", or "Around the World" in the rusted iron basketball hoop on one of the dead-end streets near Barry's house. Or, we would hide under cars in the carports close to dusk to make it challenging to find us within the shadows during a late night game of "carport tag".

Being a kid where we grew up was so easy, simple and just plain great. We really couldn't complain about our teachers, our neighbors, our incredible neighborhood and life, in general. There was always the "bully" who nobody liked and we steered clear of, but Corey would talk real big and bring his brass knuckles to the bus stop and put an end to the big mouth bullies. He had a knack for finding trouble and sometimes fights, too. Sadly, as we got older, we diverged greatly in our interests, our friend groups, and ultimately were put in completely different clicks in high school like "burnout" and "nerd". I was fine with my label but Corey took offense to "burnout" as he didn't want to use drugs or harm his body like that. His mother had gone astray taking that path in life and he was adamant not to repeat it.

The reason for many of our differences had to do with our non-custodial parents who had abandoned and wounded us deeply. We talked through these topics in counseling, individually, almost every week, yet the pain seemed to never really dissipate. Talking about it year after year, not resolving anything with his Mom and my Dad seemed to keep ripping off the band-aid and not bringing long-term solutions. Nevertheless, we kept talking to our therapist, whom we adored and trusted, and she helped us through some incredible turmoil and deep waters over many years. I was on the path of perfectionism and people-pleasing while Corey was all out living life loudly and to the fullest with a lot of anger and rebellion. He was always super tender-hearted at the root, and that was obvious to those who knew him best, but the pain for us both with broken families and absent parents took its toll on both of our souls more than could be tallied.

By my junior year in high school, I was really stressed out and in depression, however. The quest for a perfect 4.0 GPA, first chair in my two school orchestras, a place on the Varsity Track and Field Team, and many other crushing self-expectations had reached their max. I was despairing, fearful, always working more than my body could handle, and mentally, I didn't have the ability to forgive myself for any mistakes I made. The worst part about hiding unforgiveness for myself is continuing to make mistakes daily and it compounds, piling up sky high. Making excuses and blaming others for my failures to get a 100% on a test or why I was late getting somewhere was easier than accepting responsibility myself. And so the blame game began as a consequence of the suffocating gravity that perfectionism requires.

One Spring day, I was running in P.E. class last period. We were expected to run two full miles every week, outdoors on the track in under 20 minutes. I was in the Group I top level P.E. class with the highest goals and achievements required of them. Group IV was composed of kids who were mostly very overweight or addicted to video games. I was not going to be lumped in with kids in the lower groups, so I was going to keep pressing forward in class to meet every goal the teacher set for us to attain. I felt strong cramping in my right side that day as I ran which happens when you are dehydrated. That wasn't the problem, however. The pain didn't subside when I began walking.

The stress, lack of sleep, hours studying, babysitting, working, and being up for school before 5 am were taking a toll. What was happening in my body, I wondered? Could I have a bleeding ulcer like Ned from all of these life stressors? Was it a menstrual issue? Fears catapulted into my consciousness. That night, I told my Mom my concerns that this was just too much. I couldn't continue this fast-paced rat race that I was living.

"Mom, can you please check me into a mental institution for an evaluation or something? Even just *one* short week away from school, and I am sure I could rest and recover," I pleaded. That would be the answer. I just needed to get away.

"No, sweetheart, I am sure that things will look better in the morning. They always do. Get some rest, and we can talk about it some more tomorrow. I love you. Get some sleep." She said good night from my doorway, and closed the door until it was a crack of dim light from the hallway.

I fell asleep in tears again as I often did each night. I would put on a record and listen on repeat as I fell asleep to the sound of Pachelbel Canon in D or other orchestral piece. The phonograph was perched high above my bed on a painted wooden shelf Ned had built and installed for me for books, homemade bookends I made in shop class, a plant and my favorite record player. I would dance to Michael Jackson or Darryl Hall and John Oats when I was in a good mood, but something about nights, I would just lay in the dark trying to sleep listening to sad music that would evoke tears and emotions. I cried myself to sleep more nights than I could count. I had the perfect report card with straight A's, amazing friends, a path to first chair in the honors orchestra, amazing families I babysat for, and a great weekend job. Most people said I was pretty, smart, and "happy-go-lucky". What more could a 16-year-old girl want, really? Instead, the mirror lied and told me I was hideous, overweight, and too small chested for anyone to pay me attention. I would probably never find anyone to marry me. (I know now those are a stream of satan's lies designed to keep me in a desperate pit of despair.) I didn't know then that my soul was missing Jesus. His perfect love, His grace, His forgiveness, and His mercy was there all along but I didn't have anyone telling me about Him or that this free gift was available even to a broken, imperfect girl like me. When would I finally hear about Him? A chance encounter was just around the corner.

Chapter 21:   Sally

Isaiah 52:7 - "How beautiful on the mountains are the feet of those who bring good news, who proclaim peace, who bring good tidings, who proclaim salvation."

During this mental burnout school year in 1990-91, I was taking my least favorite, most hated class called Advanced Placement U.S. history. Kids today affectionately refer to it as "A-Push". We didn't have cool names back then, but I dreaded every afternoon, listening to Stormin' Norman, our teacher at the precipice of retirement, drone on about war, death, casualties, politics, and more. I was lulled to sleep by his monotone voice as he read hundreds of words he painstakingly wrote on the chalkboard for us every day. We were to copy down *every* word, *every* day and learn *every* detail. BO-ring.

Finally, we were given an assignment I could sink my teeth into. We were going to give a debate to our class regarding a political U.S. topic of our choice, ripped from the headlines, something pertinent and relevant to liven up our dull and monotonous class.

I chose the controversial topic of Roe v. Wade. This had become legal just before my birth and little did I know what a big part this played in my life, my family and in my future. (More later about how this became a prayerful heart cry for me once I became a mother!) Friends chose race relations, the Cold War with Russia and even controversy in schools. After weeks of research and preparation, the day to give my persuasive speech had finally arrived. I had practiced my speech, donned a dress and heels, and clicked into our 2nd floor History class as my friends greeted me with compliments on how professional I looked. (I liked to borrow my Mom's dresses and jewelry, and I usually looked like I was in my 20's.) I thanked them for their compliments and gathered my thoughts as well as my notecards. When Stormin' Norman called my name, I gulped a great big gulp full of nerves and fear as I picked up my white stack of lined note cards and found my way to the front of the classroom.

What am I supposed to do to calm my nerves again, imagine everyone without clothes on in the audience? Stare at their foreheads and not their eyes? Oh my, was I nervous. Another hard swallow and I plunged ahead.

"Roe v. Wade was passed in 1973 because illegal abortions were taking the lives of innocent women and girls...". I informed the class of facts, figures, details and pro-choice rhetoric that would have made any Democrat proud. With no Biblical or political foundation in my family to speak of, I simply recited all I researched and from my bleeding-heart feminist mindset of protecting women's rights. We must be allowed to choose what happens to our bodies!

Upon completing my speech, I was about to sit down when Sally stood up, pointed her finger directly towards my face and she proclaimed loudly, "You're going to church with me!" I said, "Church? Where do you go to church?" The bell rang and class was over. She proceeded to tell me where and when church services were, and I was somehow suddenly resolved to go with her that next Sunday. The unfolding of these events are so profound at just the right time when I was drowning in work, in to-do lists, in achievements and success, and in the avoidance of failure. If I were truly honest, more than the accolades of accomplishments, the fear of failing at anything or letting anyone down, obsessively motivated me more than any other driving factor. Living on the daily hamster wheel of American life left me in adrenal fatigue.

The next Sunday, I got up alone, drove myself the twenty-minute drive to a nearby suburb, and met Sally and my then best-friend Jane. We sat together with some other high school students who were incredibly warm and welcoming to me, a mere stranger. I looked around the gym at the families, men and women dressed up, musicians on stage ready to play and sing, and at the overhead screen being pulled down for lyrics. This was a school gymnasium converted to a church service on the weekends, apparently. I had never seen anything like this nor been in the presence of people seemingly so excited to come to church! My memories of the Catholic Church as a young girl with my Grandma Mueller was of a dark, somber "cathedral" and nothing like what I witnessed on this bright and cheerful Sunday morning. On the contrary, people were not shushing one another, they were hugging, clapping each other on the back, and having a rowdy good time. "What was so different?" I wondered.

We sang for over an hour, and I recognized none of the music at all. I read the names of musicians accredited in the lower right corner of the screen and had never heard even one name. I cried and cried silent tears as they rolled slowly down my cheeks during the worship. One particular song began to repeat the same chorus over and over and I found myself joining in. "Our God is an Awesome God, He reigns - from Heaven above. With wisdom, power and love, Our God is an Awesome God." The voices around me thundered and hands applauded as the crescendo of our voices swelled in that airy school auditorium that Sunday Morning. Something drew me to this song. I don't know what it was, why I felt so connected to it, but the lyrics echoed in my heart day in and day out. I cried at the simple, repetitive chorus as it filled my soul. "Our God is an Awesome God, He reigns, from Heaven above. With wisdom, power and love, our God is an Awesome God."

I sat towards the back with other high school students and tears fell down my cheeks the entirety of the service. I felt unlovable, crushed, stained and marred, and so imperfect that the God they were singing about could not possibly love me for even a moment. Jesus could not or would not have laid down His perfect life for a bruised and black soul like mine. I couldn't believe these words were really for me. (It would take years to crack through these lies to actually get to my heart and at the root of the trauma I had endured.)

"Well, what did you think?" inquired Sally after the two-hour service concluded.

"I liked it. It is not like any churches I've been to before. And I have gone to, like, 7 different denominations. I feel so different here, but I don't know why."

"So, are you coming next week?" she persisted.

"Yeah, I guess....does your family come every week?"

"Are you kidding? Every Sunday, every Wednesday night youth group, every soup kitchen day, and lock-ins...we practically live here."

"What about you, Jane, are you coming back, too?" Sally had met Jane in an Honors class that year that we didn't share, so I didn't realize that they had been getting to be good friends all semester. She had joined Sally a few weeks earlier when her parents said yes to skipping their Catholic Church service to join Sally's family. I hadn't asked my parents permission, really, I kind of told them I was going in a defiant way. In hindsight, my heart was so full of anger and rebellion, I justified my reason for going to church without asking their permission. Instead, I had proverbially stamped my foot looking for a reaction and announced, "On Sunday, I am going to church!" I was met with my Mom's calm response, "That's nice dear. Please pick up the bagels on the way home." Oh well, Jane was always the *really* good kid and actually asked permission, but I digress.

"Yes, I love coming here and just started going to youth group last week. You should come, it is amazing! Pastor Pete and his wife, Amy, are incredible and they will love you," Jane answered, convincingly.

"Okay, I only work Tuesdays and Thursdays after school at the mall right now, so I actually don't have plans at all on Wednesday nights. That could work, just getting up at 5 am for orchestra is super early. When do you guys end?"

"We start at 6 and go until 8, unless you want to hang out later and talk. It's not mandatory to stay, but you'll want to. Trust me."

"Okay, I will try to get all of my homework done in class, on the bus, or before dinner and then I'll let you know if I can make it," I optimistically told the girls after service.

That was the beginning of me getting to know Jesus. He is real. He does care. He does love us, He made us, planned us, and has plans for us. He knows us, intimately, and knows everything we are thinking. He knew I was burned out on school and life and I just couldn't pick my head up one more morning and do the same thing, trying to muddle through, and somehow put a smile on my face. It was just so exhausting, and meaningless, if I were honest. And just when I begged my Mom to send me to a mental institution the Lord sent Sally. Coincidence? No way. (My mentor, Linda, calls this a God-incidence.)

Believing in Jesus wasn't popular in my house but they let me pursue anything and everything, from church, to youth group, to lock-ins, and much more. I am sure my family thought I became a "Jesus freak", and who knows, maybe I had. I went to retreats overnight, to outdoor 4-day Jesus concerts on a 600-acre property in Western IL camping with my youth group, I stopped swearing, started listening to Christian music and radio stations only, and veered away from friends who were not headed in the right direction. I might have been accused of becoming a "holy roller", but to me, I was just, well...happy. My stress levels began to wane as I enjoyed my Christian youth group friends. They were hilarious, light-hearted, and knew how to have a ton of fun. They played sand volleyball outside the church and at the beach on Saturdays, they went to Six Flags, and watched movies together. We played games like "Spoons" and "Jenga" at our pastor's house on weekend nights and spent a lot of time singing and learning God's Word together. We had picnics at the beach near Chicago and played "Chinese fire drill" on the way there in multiple cars (if you grew up in the '80's or '90's you are laughing right now).

Junior and Senior year with these friends made all the difference. Next, deciding where to go to college, navigating life transitions, saying good-bye to the dearest people in my life, and heading off into the unknown would be another chapter. Suffice it to say, for now, having the structure of church twice a week, amazing friends to talk to about all of the hard things in life, people to study Calculus with when I was drowning in confusion, and people to laugh with was priceless.

Chapter 22:   The Hamster Wheel

Isaiah 40:7-8 - "The grass withers and the flower fades: because the Spirit of the Lord blows upon it, surely the people are grass. The grass withers, the flower fades, but the Word of the Lord will stand forever."

What I did not realize during the next several years that unfolded was that it is so much easier to "follow Jesus" with a group of people who are living the Christian lifestyle, too. Avoiding many of life's temptations was easier when you have friends who are committed to living the same way.

Leaving high school that next year and heading into college, I was resolved to remain pure before marriage, abstain from alcohol and substances, and still maintain my moratorium on swearing. I had a squeaky clean boyfriend from my home church in Wheeling, Illinois who was kind, funny, supportive, and was very steadfast on maintaining his Christian lifestyle. His example was a blessing to me and I was very fortunate to date him for two years.

As a teenage girl who was both very impressionable and social, I wanted to do what the Lord wanted and being with the youth group friends at the time, it was just an easy, new way of life. The old has gone away, and behold, the new has come! (Paul tells us this in II Corinthians, describing

salvation.) What I didn't know then, and painfully learned later, is that my

surrender had not happened. I wanted to read the Bible, go to Bible study,

sing worship music, and commit to a life with Him (my observations of the

American form of Christianity), however, whether I just missed it in a sermon,

or didn't connect the Truth with my reality, I had not laid down any idols.

College life caused me to be confronted with and devastated by my

idolatry. The pain and rejection that pursued me from childhood overtook my

heart as my life took many forks in the road at points of trauma. Satan uses

his wiles to implant lies into each crisis moment to cause the person to believe

that lie, then be fed another, and begin to move away from the Lord's identity

and closer to a life of bondage to those lies instead of Freedom in Christ Jesus.

Jesus offers true forgiveness from things we have done so that we are

alleviated from sins we have committed and the record of wrongs is

obliterated. He tells us that he casts our sins as far as the east is from the west

(Psalm 103). We do not need to live under guilt, shame or condemnation,

either (Romans 8:1).

The first lie I believed at three-years-old was that my parents' divorce

was my fault. If I had been a better daughter, kinder, better mannered or more obedient, this would never have happened. And the deadly spiral began. My brain and heart were reprogrammed to believe perfectionism and people-pleasing was my responsibility for keeping relationships in tact and that I had to work tirelessly at them to keep them healthy and well. That is never the job of a person. Praise the Lord, only He is capable of sustaining people and truly bringing them joy, hope, peace, forgiveness, and reconciliation. The rest of the lies I began believing grew more intricate and fierce as I obediently paid homage to the first.

I was looking for accolades, beauty, body image, perfect grades, and a stellar reputation to be the answer to my life's quest. Eureka! Then, I will find happiness! Instead of knowing my identity in Christ Jesus, as His blood-bought adopted daughter, which negates the need to "prove" myself worthy or earn credits towards some hard-to-reach goal, I was already seen in God's eyes as loved and chosen. I never heard this message, or perhaps I "listened" to this message, but never received it for myself. It would be almost two decades before I could grasp how deep, how high, how long and how wide is the love of Jesus and it is truly for me.

Weighed down in a world of self-righteousness to be the "best Christian" I could be, I was relying on will power and self-determination to achieve each of these goals for myself. I was back to the "hamster-wheel" of life scenario that I found myself in that P.E. class years before when I evaluated my life and believed going to a mental hospital for respite over a week or two would solve my problems.

What I didn't realize in high school or in college, is that my problems would come with me. My problem was me. My incorrect attitude and false beliefs about myself, about who God is, His plan for my life, and the Hope that is found only in Him were running me into the ground once more. I was depleted, mentally exhausted, and running out of idols to chase to possibly find the all-elusive "life's purpose." I was trapped in a monotonous cycle of get up, perform, wear myself out doing so, go to bed, repeat. I was stuck.

I would have been diagnosed with mild depression at the time. I see the pattern of these cycles in my adolescent years, high school, college and even some winters into adulthood. What I soon learned is that I was not the only one. Someone near and dear to me had been dealing with the weight of the world and lies from the enemy from before I was born.

Chapter 23:   Resurrection

John 11:25 - "I am the Resurrection and the Life, He that believes in me, though he were dead, yet he shall live," Jesus said.

While I was busy raising Lilly and Marcus, running a Purchasing Department with eight employees, and trying to be the perfect employee, I still tried to be a good wife, mother and daughter. The demands on my time and my lack of sleep with Marcus not sleeping through the night for well over 13 months wore me down to the nub. I worked 9 plus hours per day, commuted 10 hours per week, dropped the kids at our babysitter's home, then rushed home, made dinner, gave the kids baths, tried to finish my Bible study or current book, and then crashed into bed each night. There was very little time for me and James and definitely no time for me to really explore what "made me tick". Life was going Mach 5 with my hair on fire, as my employees liked to call our fast-past corporate culture, and there was little time for introspection or self-correction. This was definitely not the path I thought my life would take after meeting Jesus for the first time in my late high school years.

Did I really have any concept of who God is? Did He want this rat race for me? Was He content with me being discontent? Is this all the Christian life is? Going to church, reading Bible studies at home, making notes in my

margins with dates and "a-ha" moments, and barely sleeping enough to

remember what day it is in the morning? There is no way that Jesus came to

earth, lived a perfect, sinless life in a human body, willingly laid His life down

for us and then was brutally tortured and killed for us to barely hang on by

our fingernails. No way. What was I missing?

As these days after Marcus' near death experience went into the

rearview mirror, I began to find more co-workers who knew the Lord. There

was a sweet Filipino man named Joe Reyes who I would occasionally bump into

on a project we were working on together for his client. I began to see the

peace in his demeanor and the kindness in his tone as he spoke to others. He

was gentle and so in love with his wife. This seemed so rare in this face-paced

beauty and success-crazed American society. I was intrigued by what was so

different about him.

One day in discussing the delivery dates of metal tubing for his urgent

client's cosmetic display, Joe casually mentioned a marriage retreat that would

be hosted in a month at a church in the same town as our manufacturing

company. I asked him about some of the details and he gave me the dates,

cost, location and conference host, Moody Bible Institute. As a very well-known and reputable midwest church with a legacy of sending pastors and missionaries off to dozens of countries for ministry, I assumed we could trust the chosen speakers to come breathe life into James' and my dead marriage.

The weekend quickly approached and my parents offered to watch Lilly and Marcus both Friday night and all day Saturday so that we could attend the 2-day conference. James and I were like an awkward estranged couple going into this foreign place teeming with 1000 other married people. I scanned the crowd wondering if it were obvious what a terrible state of disconnection we were in, or if we could fake it and blend in for two days and simply sit under this teaching to begin the healing we so desperately needed in our marriage. Could I cry in public and not care about all the strangers around us? The hollow ache in my heart was so deep and forlorn I didn't know how much hope there really was for me and James. We were radically different in *every* way from calling the sky the right color, to raising kids, to priorities, hobbies, dreams in life, birth family dynamics, our ideas of conflict resolution, stewarding money, disciplining children, whether or not to have pets, and every other imaginable conversation point. How could we have wandered so far back into this lonely, isolated territory after that joyful year of expecting and giving birth to sweet Baby Lilly? Simple, what divided us was never discussed, resolved or healed. We just simply kept moving forward.

A worship team took the stage and began to sing a song that rattled my soul to the core. An anointed voice I had never heard before sang the haunting lyrics of a song called, "Resurrection". I sat in silence. I was stunned. I cried silently as my soul connected with the message of this song. The depth of her story set to song coiled itself around every nano millimeter of my heart that night. This was where I was treading water in that season. Dead, lost, lonely, despairing, discouraged, exhausted, lifeless, and pretty hopeless was where I found myself regarding my marriage to James. I closed my eyes and let Nicol Sponberg sing over us the Truth of resurrection and how life can come again after death. The flat-lining soul can be shocked to life by the agape Love of Our Lord Jesus and His resurrection power. I wept silent tears and instead of feeling cold, disjointed, and in utter despair, a crack through the cold winter soil of my heart sprouted a green seed of HOPE. I will never forget that moment. Observing James, he may not have felt it, experienced it, or been set on a new path by this moment, but the important thing was that I was. There was a sun most assuredly coming up over the horizon. A penetrating light at the end of a very long, dark and ominous tunnel. There was

resurrection coming.

(The lyrics are here for you to read, soak in, enjoy and richly read. I

encourage you to listen to a version of this song on any source you can find. If

this is where you are in your personal journey to find meaning and

fulfillment, to gain hope that life will improve or your marriage be healed, for

your heart to be resurrected after a crushing loss, after losing a person so

dear you cannot explain in words, let the Truth of Jesus' Hope flood your soul

as you listen to these words.)

Resurrection by Nicol Sponberg   *(2004)*
> *"I'm at a loss for words, there's nothing to say*
> *sit in silence wondering what led me to this place*
>
> *How did my heart become so lifeless and cold*
>
> *Where did the passion go?*
>
> *When all my efforts seem like chasing wind*
>
> *I've used up all my strength and there's nothing left to give*
>
> *I've lost the feeling and I'm numb to the core*
>
> *I can't fake it anymore.*
>
> *Here I am at the end I'm in need of resurrection*

Only You can take this empty shell and raise it from the dead

What I've lost to the world what seems far beyond redemption

You can take the pieces in Your hand and make me whole again,

You speak and all creation falls to its knees

You raise Your hand and calm the waves of the raging sea

You have a way of turning winter to spring

Make something beautiful out of all this suffering

Here I am once again I'm in need of resurrection

Only You can take this empty shell and raise it from the dead

What I've lost to the world what seems far beyond redemption

You can take the pieces in Your hand and make me whole again,

You have a way of turning winter to spring

Make something beautiful out of all this suffering

Here I am at the end I'm in need of resurrection

Only You can take this empty shell and raise it from the dead

What I've lost to the world what seems far beyond redemption

You can take the pieces in Your hand and make me whole again"

Leaving that night, I had a whisper in my soul that God was with us and He saw. He knew, and He wasn't letting our marriage perish. We might have to fight against hell, but it wasn't going down for the count that easily. Just like the night that Marcus almost lost his tiny newborn life to the jaws of death, I had heard the Heavenly promise, "This is not his day." We drove home mostly in silence that night knowing an 8-hour day of being under the marriage microscope awaited us in the morning. I'm certain neither of us was looking forward to it.

That cold Saturday winter morning, we drove the 30-minutes back to the church with the nameless, faceless married couples who were back at it with us for round 2. Upon looking for new seats that morning, Joe and his lovely wife, Sonia, came over to say hello. I greeted him, met her for the first time and introduced them both to James. We thanked them for inviting us and found seats away from them and their church friends in the cacophonous sanctuary. It was easy to hide amongst hundreds of others, but what I didn't realize at that moment was that neither of us were hiding anything from God. He saw our plight, our shattered hearts, and the yearning we both had to be "whole". Sadly, we had zero understanding of how to go from where we were to that place of a unified and joyful marriage.

Dr. Crawford and Karen Loritts soon took the stage to greet us on that cold, bleak morning and light streamed into our hearts in the message they imparted to the hungry congregation. They spoke on marriage not as a piece of paper, legal agreement or contract. Marriage is a sacred covenant. (What?) We heard them correctly, it is a covenant. It is a long-standing, permanent forging of two parties who willingly agree to embark on the marriage relationship not only in the eyes of one another and family, but most importantly, in the eyes of Our Heavenly Father. He forges covenants, He brings people together, He introduces the gift of His perfect Son Jesus to them and allows them to choose a forever love story to unfold as both man and wife. Each surrenders their own will to their Abba, Daddy, and walk towards holiness in their union. None of this had ever been revealed to me or James before. We thought that marriage was a man-made institution and in that year, cohabitation probably superseded the number of married couples in America, tragically. We didn't learn this in church, or Sunday school, or in premarital pastoral counseling, or in Christian books we read. How did we miss this vital teaching about the most important relationship on earth outside of family?

Heading out of the morning session, we were asked to go on an indoor picnic with our spouse where we would have a little "basket" with red-white checkered napkins, sandwiches and other light lunch fare, and a packet of conversation starters. As we found a small but quiet space to sit Indian style on the roughly carpeted cement floor in the children's wing, I felt like we were utter and total strangers going on a blind date. Who was this man I was sitting across from that I once adored, looked forward to talking to on the phone, bragged about to my friends, and found so ruggedly handsome? I feel like he is a fraction of that man today, and I don't even know what to say to him! I felt vulnerable and somewhat naked emotionally as we sat down and were supposed to "talk" for one hour. What could we possibly say for that long and not be allowed to talk about kids, pets, family, finances, or the "to-do" list?

"Okay, do you want the ham or the turkey sandwich?" James asked, holding two sandwiches out in front of him over the red-and-white checkered paper cloth.

"I would prefer the turkey, if that is okay with you," I replied carefully.

Unwrapping the food slowly, we looked at each other without an iota of conversation and I hesitated praying out loud before we ate. Closing my eyes briefly, I thanked the Lord for our lunch and asked him to do a miracle to soften our hearts.

"We are supposed to ask these questions if we are stuck on what to say," I ventured, pulling out a small paper packet of random questions. "What is the most embarrassing thing that ever happened in elementary school?"

"Oh, this is gonna be so awkward and he probably won't answer any of them," I thought, "How can these questions strangers don't even ask one another save our estranged and distant marriage?"

Oddly enough, James got a minor smile on his face as he reminisced about the events of childhood. Soon, he was divulging a memory from years gone by that actually caused me to say something like, "Really? That happened to you? I never heard that story!"

Next, he pulled a card and asked me a random question about my school and favorite friend I had in 5th grade. "I went to Booth Tarkington School in Wheeling, Illinois. That year I was new to my school and didn't have a best friend yet. The next year, Jenae moved to our school and she was for sure my BFF." These people must have known what they were doing, because James and I hadn't had a light-hearted conversation like this in months, maybe in a year or more. I felt the ice melting and we slowly began to warm up to being in each other's company. The rest of the cards were left in the rubber band as we finished up discussing our two fond memories and then just simply began to, well, talk. Some of our words were forced or felt foreign as we had to plan our sentences carefully so as to not step on one another's feelings. Other comments came out with less effort or premeditation. By the time the hour wrapped up, we felt a little more human than when we arrived and walking back into the giant sanctuary felt slightly more inviting. The afternoon was going to be life-giving, I was certain of it.

Dr. Gary Chapman, famous author of the "Five Love Languages" and a plethora of other titles, was our keynote speaker. Boy were we in for an hour of lots of laughter! He humorously described the common marital pairings of the "Babbling Brook" and the "Dead Sea", two complementary personality types who simply met one another's socialization needs as one couldn't think of anything to say and absorbed everything they heard and the other was full of incessant, perpetual chatter. Well, that describes the two of us to a "tee" and I bet you can guess who is who. I laughed and laughed, looking over at James who occasionally shrugged his shoulders and might have even copped a few dimpled inadvertent smiles on occasion. The day was looking up.

At the end of the two-day marriage "retreat", we had a better understanding of what we were facing, where we truly were, and a vague idea of where we were headed. The revolutionary "Truth Bomb" of our marriage being a covenant, not simply a legal contract in the state of IL and the eyes of citizens became a watershed moment for us. Divorce was not an option, and we both unspokenly agreed in our hearts that we are not giving up. Second, we knew that there was some real truth in the personality types we heard described and our differences are what drew each other in like magnets almost a decade earlier, and those are actually strengths we need to draw from instead of point the finger at. Next, we heard the repeated message that the Lord was at the core of a successful and long-lasting joyful marriage, so our only choice really, was to choose to place Him there by our own volition. I already had a budding relationship with Jesus and had to choose to make Him the master of our marriage and to guide my every decision. James was still not in the same place, spiritually, but this weekend was sure to give him food for thought. One thing was for certain, the iceberg had been found, the tip had broken off, and we were beginning to swim in warmer waters. There was hope.

Chapter 24: Daisy's Secret

Psalm 40:1-2 - "I waited patiently for the LORD, He inclined His ear to me and heard my cry. He brought me up out of the pit, out of the miry clay and put my feet upon a rock so I could stand."

Around this same year, as I was overwhelmed with life, commitments, daily activities, and in survival mode, Daisy was hitting a wall and tried hard to hide it for years. Looking back years later at pictures, she would point out her expressionless countenance in photographs and tell us, "See, you can see it in my face here. I was in depression then."

The announcement came a year-and-a-half after our marriage retreat and hit me like an atomic bomb. How could I have missed all of the telltale signs of depression? I studied Psychology for 4 years in college, went to counseling for mild depression for over 6 years, and spent a lot of time with my mother. How in the world could I have been so oblivious to her mental state? The simple answer, she had a great way of hiding it and my lifestyle kept me fairly self-absorbed.

The call came from Ned to my cell phone while the 8 of us were on a McKnight Family vacation in Myrtle Beach, SC. I sat on the yellow hotel sofa in utter disbelief as I heard his voice on the other end of the line. He divulged that my Mom was severely depressed. I was in disbelief. I felt helpless so far away from them.

Next, Evangelina called to share what she experienced being with my Mom. With rapid-fire back-to-back phone calls, I was seeking instant solutions and rescue for my sweet mother who was drowning in a morass of self-deprecating lies. Thoughts like, "You have no value, no one will miss you, when you die, hardly anyone will care, and life will be better for those you love when you are gone" were allegedly bombarding her waking thoughts. What I didn't have a grasp on in 2007 that I am well-versed in today, is that these classic spiritual warfare lies are used by satan to torment millions of people. They are well-worn, used up, tired, and defeated lies that seem new to the "victim" and as brain chemistry is altered, the person pulls away from those they love, and get isolated with these viscous lies, and the torture escalates. Either the person becomes clinically depressed, often suicidal, wishing they were out of their mental anguish, or wants to go isolate and hide. Sometimes, all of the above occurs. My Mom had sunk to a place I didn't know was humanly possible for the most fun, effervescent, vivacious woman I had ever known. She had ideas that gave birth to more ideas, energy to spare, a spark that easily lit even the most lifeless and dead situations, and she ran circles around most everyone on the planet. She was, after all, Daisy Jane, one-of-a-kind.

Eight hundred miles from her, I sat on that yellow, now obnoxious couch, wishing I were just 3 miles down the road, which was the short distance we lived apart in Illinois. Three days away from our 14-hour drive home, I was feeling like a trapped animal.

On the call to Evangelina, she shared incredibly pertinent details. She had called my mom to ask her to come over for a free pedicure a few days earlier. This was Evangelina's gracious way of both blessing people with a tangible gift, physically (leaving them with beautifully polished toes), and spiritually by ministering to their hearts. Evangelina is a great listener, extremely compassionate, kind, gentle, humble and wise. She knows when to hold her tongue and listen, and when the Holy Spirit is prompting her to speak a nugget of Godly wisdom that the person needs to hear in their plight. My Mom was like a second mom to her, although her own family knew the Lord and mine did not, they lived almost 3 minutes apart and had spent hours and hours together with our 4 small children over the years. Daisy trusted and loved her very much, so at the sound of her voice, she willingly drove the short mile or two to Evangelina's front door. Her boys played in the back room while Daisy soaked her feet in the portable foot massaging tub full of warm water and a fragrant solution to soften her skin. As she soaked, they talked. Evangelina prayed continuously as she listened, and Daisy confessed her dark thoughts. Evangelina reminded my Mom of Jesus' perfect life and sacrifice and asked her to give her life to Him that day. Daisy said "Yes", in the moment. She prayed a prayer that many Christians today would affectionately call, "The Sinner's Prayer". Daisy verbally repeated after my sweet friend as she stared down at the carpet, feeling numb. Seemingly, no relationship change took place, no light flooded her heart, and days later, the darkness got even darker for her.

James, the kids and I raced home (we didn't tell them why at their young ages) from Myrtle Beach early the morning of our planned departure, and all I could ruminate on was my Mom's fragile mental state. What would she be saying and believing when we arrived? Would I be too late? How bad were things? Arriving at our house, we unpacked, called Ned and asked about my Mom. He was furtive about certain details with her within earshot, but we got the gist that she was in a super hard place, mentally. We wanted to come over and encourage her and talk, but that would have to wait until tomorrow,

Monday morning, after the kids' already scheduled annual pediatrician appointments. Little did we know, time was of the essence.

Early the next morning, I rose early as usual, packed the diaper bag and some essentials with snacks and sippy cups, and drove the 10-minutes to our pediatric office that had cared for both kids since their birth. The doctors here knew Marcus' aspiration incident and cautioned many parents of newborns, when graduating to solid foods, to be careful to give them morsel sized pieces to prevent choking. We had heard the stories from two family friends in our preschool that Marcus's case became a springboard for this doctor's warning parents at their baby's 1-year checkups to prevent a tragedy from occurring in other babies.

Arriving in the familiar parking lot, I was completely oblivious to what kind of day lay before me. We sat in the waiting room completing the obligatory paperwork and waited until the kids' names were called by a pink scrub-wearing young nurse at the hallway door. Taking all of our things and both kids down the corridor to a brightly decorated exam room, Lilly would be examined first, being the oldest. In between children's check-ups, I got another call from Ned, which was highly unusual. He rarely ever talked on the phone, and when he called, it was nearly always an emergency. He told me my Mom was talking about death and being "out of agony". Sadly, I had to tell him where I was for the next 20 minutes or so, and that I would drop the kids with Evangelina and rush immediately over. My mind was spinning and I had to ground myself in the moment, remembering to engage with the doctor and get through the two check-ups. No, I had no concerns about their growth, health, development, and we would see them next summer.

Racing to the parking lot with the diaper bag and kids in tow, I buckled them into their car seats and explained they were going to have a "play date" with Miss Evangelina's boys for a few hours while I hung out with Grandma and Grandpa. As I pulled up her driveway and thanked her for the last minute babysitting request, we prayed outside of earshot of the kids. "Dear God, save Daisy and let her know your immense love for her. Let her come to know you truly as her Lord and Savior and set her free, in Jesus' Name. Amen." "Amen!" I agreed and rushed to my idling car in her driveway.

Being less than three minutes from my folks' house, I remember gripping the steering wheel, crying and praying verses that leapt out of my heart, "Lord, you have allowed me to come to my Mom's side 'for such a time as this' like Esther prayed, I need you to fill me with your Spirit and with the right words to say. Use me, Lord, like never before. I am so thankful we made it

home last night on time. Please save my Mom and save her life! In Jesus'
Name!"

Pulling up to their 2-story home, I was filled with anxious urgency as I
threw the car hastily in park. I ran to their front steps and barely knocked on
the front door. Walking into the atrium, I slid off my shoes and heard voices in
the living room. What I was about to see, I was ill-prepared for. My Mom sat
upright almost motionless on the dark maroon couch. Her eyes had lost all
color as had her pallid cheeks. She looked nothing like my Mom. I heard a
whisper from her lips that sounded nothing like her, either. What had
happened in the 9 days we were on vacation? I guess the better question was,
what had been simmering all of the time prior to us leaving town that I hadn't
recognized?

"Living is just too painful. I can't do this anymore. It is just too hard,"
she mustered energy to say.

I was stunned speechless. I was looking at a woman who was a shell of
herself and I didn't know where this was stemming from. I looked at Ned, and
I prayed for wisdom before I spoke. What could I say?

"Mom, you do have a lot to live for. This is extremely hard right now
because your thoughts are telling you things that make living so painful. Ned

and I love you, James, Lilly and Marcus adore you, and we are here for you. I don't know how this is for you and how horrible this depression has been, but we are going to help you in every way that we can." I hugged her rigid and unmoving figure leaning stoically on the couch.

Gesturing to Ned to join me in the kitchen, I slowly arose and walked a few steps to the right and onto the kitchen tile. "I thought she was in a bad place, but this is not what I expected at all. Did something else happen?"

"I don't know, she just keeps going on and on about how this is too hard and she doesn't want to go on," Ned said despairingly, his face a sickly shade of gray.

"At this point, she is a risk to herself, and we need to get someone else involved. She might be angry with us, but we have to think about her well-being. This isn't her talking at all!"

"I called her therapist and asked to come in this morning as soon as there is an emergency opening. We are leaving here in less than an hour. I am going to sit in on the session with her."

"Do you want me to come with you?"

"No, I think it's best that your Mom and I are alone with her, and I'm hoping she will offer help to us. I don't know what to do. Your Mom is everything to me."

"Ned, this is terrible, but she is going to be okay. She has gotten through dozens of horrible things in her life and she is a fighter and comes out the other side. I am staying here until you have to leave. The kids are fine with Evangelina until you leave, then I will pick them up and take them home to James. I will be available all day. No matter what. James and Evangelina are praying, our church friends are praying now and the Lord does *not* want anything to happen to her. He loves her."

I sat with my Mom, reaching up to hold her hand as I sat on the carpeting near her feet. "I love her so much, Lord...you have to heal her mind and remove all these lies that satan is taunting her with. This is despicable and wicked and I cannot stand by and let her be ravaged like this! This is NOT my Mom! The enemy is a liar and we need to silence him right now! In Jesus' Name!" I prayed in utter desperation under my breath as I sat there floundering for what to say.

Looking at the clock, Ned looked tenderly at his wife and gently said, "We need to get to that appointment now, sweetheart." Ned gathered up their things and put them into the car before walking my Mom gently to the garage. He helped her into the passenger seat and I stayed, my eyes fixed on them until they slowly pulled away from the curb. I waved dejectedly as I watched them disappear. "I love you and I won't stop fighting!" I said to myself, crying, breaking into sobs.

The therapist suggested my Mom be checked into a behavior unit as soon as possible to ensure she was in a safe place and got the observation and medication necessary to allow her brain chemistry to rebalance itself again. Her neurotransmitters were so far depleted from her naturally hyper and highly energetic self, I knew that although medication is not what she wanted, this might be the only way to restore her to normal thought patterns. The 10-day stay seemed like months as she was only allowed a few visitors for a few fleeting hours each week. Ned and I went together once or twice, and I read to her, hugged her, prayed for her, and shared stories I had hoped were encouraging. She was unable to receive my news as encouragement, and looking back, I was probably talking far too much and listening too little. I needed to show support, simply sit, show her love, and accept that this was currently extremely hard. Our family needed to all rally around her and support her like never before.

Friends sent cards, texts, emails, and left messages when they heard that she needed prayer. Hundreds loved her, and the few that knew, reached out and were super supportive and compassionate.

On one of these one-hour visitor's days, we ended early afternoon and Ned suggested taking me to his grandchildrens' favorite restaurant. They affectionately called it "The Sucker Restaurant", as he made sure to get them a sucker from the cashier's desk after every meal there. Today was much more somber. There would be no suckers, and there were no boisterous children or chatter, either. We had a frank heart-to-heart about my Mom, life, death, and I finally mustered up the courage to ask about where he stood in his faith in Jesus.

"I know Jesus is my Lord and Savior," Ned quickly quipped, matter-of-factly.

"What? You do?" I thought to myself. "Why have you never said this in like, two decades to me?" I was stunned at his pronouncement.

"Okay, that is great to hear. So what about my Mom?"

"She has her own beliefs and I have always let her have them. Nothing is going to come between me and your Mom. Never," Ned vowed. And he meant it. They had been through hell and high water and despite the enemy's most strategic tactics to kill, steal and destroy them as individuals, and their marriage, they had never been torn asunder! This is a huge testimony to the Lord's faithfulness. He knew that within their marriage, they served to heal one another in beautiful ways. They were able to be transparent about the hardships life had thrown at them, the people who betrayed them, their parents who tragically failed them, and their spouses who had not been able to fulfill their marriage vows. Their marriage was solid and Ned's vow was unwavering.

"So, how are you doing, truly?" I inquired of my stepfather.

"I don't have time to think about that right now, I have to be strong for your Mom. When I hear from the doctor, I will let you know your Mom's discharge date. If I need anything, I will let you know," he said, intentionally changing the subject. Ned was never good about talking about himself.

"Is there anything else the doctor shared with you that I should know?" I inquired.

"Nothing I can think of. I brought you up to date. Tell James and the kids I love them," he hugged me longer than usual as we departed.

"I will," I promised, waving as he walked to his car. I unlocked my silver SUV and got in, almost numb. What does he mean Jesus is his Lord and

Savior? We have been talking to him about the things of God for years and he has never responded in any positive way. We have prayed fervently and tearfully hundreds of times for them both, even with the kids. I tried to process this new information as I wound my way through West Dundee into Carpentersville and north towards home. The next week of Daisy's release would be telling as to what the future held for our small extended family.

Chapter 25:   James' Journey

James 1:2 - "My brothers, consider it all joy when you meet trials of various kinds."

James had more trials bombarding his life within a three year span than most of the people I knew combined. First, his daughter begins having seizures at 12 weeks of age as a brand new father, then his son at the tender of age of 12 months old was choking to death in the ER in front of him, his bosses embezzled millions putting the company out of business, and his closest business partners betrayed him after forging a brand new venture together.

"This is a lot to take, Lord, even for James. I don't know how much more he can manage," was a common admission I had in this very trying season. Unfortunately, he was not quite in the clear yet. There was another serious hindrance to vanquish, and this one hit closer to home.

Meanwhile, my Bible study ladies at the Methodist church were fervently praying for James' salvation. They prayed for him to be humbled, turn to the Lord, and give his life to Him once and for all, willingly, without reservation. We met each Wednesday night for a study called "W.O.W.", an acronym for Women of the Word. The ages ranged from me being the

youngest member, around 29 years of age, up to a sweet woman named,

Avalee, who was 79 years-old. She was a staple in the church with her husband

of over 50 years, and I adored her. She reminded me of my now deceased

sweet Grandma Mueller who raised me for two years, took me to church,

taught me the rosary and about proper manners. Avalee and these women

were steadfast in their prayers, uplifting with their words, and the kind of

"mothers" and "grandmothers" in the faith that an ignorant young mother like

me needed, desperately. They were a blessing from Heaven!

After being in the Bible study with them for about two years each week

("Jesus *never* takes the summers off!" our fearless leader Cecelia would often

say), the fall was upon us. We had constantly changing prayer lists emailed

and spoken between us all week long. None of us were at a lack of requests

regarding sickness, prodigal family members, job changes, financial needs,

marriage troubles, moving, and much more. They prayed for all four of us

and I prayed for them. These were some of the most incredible years of my

Christian walk as I was learning what I missed out on for so many years.

The kids were into a more traditional school routine with preschool in

the mornings and day care in the afternoons. James was fastidious about being their chauffeur while I had a very demanding corporate job that took me away from home before 7 am each day until after 5:15 pm. He would shuttle them to the babysitter's after Noah's Ark preschool in our church to get them a foundation in Christian community and then to a woman's home who simply adored watching children. It was during this busy time in August, he noticed there was something odd about the tingling sensation in his face that was increasingly obvious and bothersome. It was nothing he had ever experienced before. Not knowing the root cause, he felt compelled to have it investigated by a doctor.

I looked through my company's medical benefits and found an in-network provider that would be able to do not only an annual routine check-up, but also run blood work to see if anything was amiss. After the first appointment, the bloodwork showed that his calcium levels were excessively high, and they suggested he be referred to an endocrinologist. Apparently, the glands that regulate calcium might be overworking to put too much into his bloodstream and the tingling and other odd symptoms seemed to be a possible culprit. He had kidney stones a few times, and this was dropping more pieces of the puzzle into place as the parathyroid gland was producing an excess of hormones which secretes calcium. His previous kidney stones had been tested and shown to be composed of pure calcium.

James was referred to a specialist, immediately, and their first open appointment for new patients was a few weeks away. Seeing as how we were really nervous about what was happening, days passed by like weeks. The doctors were not concerned upon the initial call, therefore, he was stuck waiting. Finally, September rolled around and he drove alone to the visit as I dropped the kids at daycare and went to work. I don't remember the thoughts I had circling in this season except to say that soon, my level of concern skyrocketed to fear.

After the first visit, they opted to run a scan that would check the size of James' parathyroid glands which are 4 small glands hidden near the thyroid responsible for the calcium levels in the body, amongst other important functions. Unlike some organs, they can be removed, if necessary, and a person can live with one or more missing glands. The remaining organs are designed by the Lord to compensate for the missing glands and continue to regulate calcium, phosphorus and magnesium in the bones and blood.

Following the appointment, we waited for days to receive results. We both felt so young and in some regards, immortal being only in our early '30's.

We worked out 5-6 times per week, ate relatively healthy meals, and tried to avoid all artificial ingredients in most of our diet. We steered clear of carcinogens, intentionally, whether smoking, artificial sweeteners, and dozens more so that we would have the cleanest possible household and hopefully, our bodies as well. We were in full agreement about our kids living in a "safe" home without harmful chemicals and substances being introduced to their vulnerable and innocent bodies.

As the days ticked by, a phone call came from the doctors' office leaving a troubling and cursory message on our answering machine. The woman who called could not disclose information over the phone regarding James' results. She said the tests came back as "abnormal", however, no further details were disclosed. I relayed the message to James. Hearing that there was something abnormal on the PET scan they performed was very troubling to us. I had a really hard time focusing my thoughts on anything else. Was this a tumor? Was it cancer? Why couldn't they tell us on the phone?

James called the office, and the only consolation they could offer was scheduling a second appointment for the following week to give him the information face-to-face. They refused to share medical details over the phone. Six days away. How is it possible for six days to feel like a month? Why would they refuse to allow him to call in for further clarification?

That week, I began to see an answer to my five years of praying for my husband's salvation. I had the Methodist ladies praying, a few coworkers I confided in, and Evangelina. First, I noticed he lay in bed with his hands folded. Was he praying? I had never seen this before! Another night, I saw him kneeling at the bedside. Surely, he was praying, yes! Within this 2-3 week period, near the day of announcing "the diagnosis", he was lying where I could not even see him anymore! He must be flat on the floor praying! My heart raced with expectation that indeed, he must be reaching out to God in prayer during this tenuous time.

That next Wednesday study, I brought the news to the ladies, exuberantly. I had grabbed a tiny scrap of envelope and written out the dates to announce the progression of James' surrender. I reported the chicken scratch I hurriedly recorded on the white envelope: *"September 5th, laying in bed with hands folded, September 7th, kneeling next to the bed before going to sleep, September 11th, on the floor out of sight before getting into bed (laying prostrate in prayer maybe?)".*

They celebrated with me! We knew no matter what the news shared during next week's appointment, God is with us, holding us, and I have my sisters to stand with me no matter what life throws our way.

I was encouraged by these new behaviors I was seeing in James, but I had a high level of fear. I had a hard time hiding my emotions from my closest co-workers, so I shared a little and they were checking in with me periodically during that season. These friends showed compassion during many years of hardships our young family had recently endured.

The next Friday in September rolled around and James drove solely to the second appointment to find out "the news". Waiting at work was hard. It was like taking a breath at the beginning of the day and holding it until his phone call came.

"It's not cancer," James' reassuring voice said from the other end of the cell phone.

"Thank you, JESUS!" I ran out into the parking lot on the call and screamed!!! This was the best news I had heard all year! "Praise GOD! That is awesome news! What did they say?"

"They don't know why the parathyroid gland is 110 times the normal size, almost a golf ball, but there is no tumor, no cancer, however, they want to perform surgery."

"Oh," I said, swallowing. I was in a bit of shock. "Okay...when?"

"They have an opening in December, that is really the earliest they can schedule me. I know it is a really long wait. I am going to tell them to go ahead."

"Wow. We just got the best news and this feels a little bit like a gut punch. Okay. I will take off work whenever it is. Of course I want to be there for you and with you. Wow. This is good news but not quite what I expected. Are you concerned about the surgery?"

"Not really, you know me, my oldest friend, Dave, is a surgeon and he does this kind of thing five times a day. There should be nothing complicated about it. Just a quick removal of the gland which is emitting mass quantities of calcium into my system. Once it is removed, the symptoms will soon subside. I will be grateful for that. Of course, I am a little scared as I have never been through anything like this in my life. You know that. We can talk more at home. I called you first. I want to call my folks and Dave to ask about the procedure. He will put my mind at ease and probably crack a bunch of jokes, too. I'll tell you what he says. I bet it will be minimally invasive."

"Thank you for calling me first...yes, please let me know what he says as soon as you talk to him. I'll be home with the kids around quarter to six. I love you. Okay, bye, Honey."

And like that, James didn't have cancer. I praised God again in that parking lot on that warm September day and just stood in awe of answered prayers. Oh, God, we are so thankful!

Chapter 26:   God's Adopted Son

Ephesians 1:5 - "God predestined us unto the adoption of children by Jesus Christ to Himself, according to the good pleasure of His will."

After the news about not having cancer and James' prolonged nights of praying at our bedside, there were some definite changes in him. I saw a softening of his demeanor, he became more patient with me, and there was something else. He seemed to want to spend more time together as a family. Ever the meticulous housekeeper, he was always the one vacuuming, cleaning, organizing, and straightening for hours each week. He rarely sat down to relax except to watch sports. Meanwhile, I was playing with the kids, taking them on bike rides, to the park, the pool, to see friends, and offer socialization with kids their ages. This was an incredibly high priority for me while they were toddlers and into elementary school. My closest newfound friend, Evangelina, was a dream come true and her two kids were just weeks and days apart from our two kiddos. They were best friends and had the time of their lives.

One Sunday afternoon, James' lack of activity in the house had me very curious. We had gone to church and had lunch, and invited a mom and her sweet 4-year-old daughter, Christy, over to play games with me and Lilly while Marcus was taking his long afternoon nap. We played in our living room, far from the upstairs where Marcus would be undisturbed by us playing a fun and familiar board game called "Zootopia". Lilly and Christy were great friends from our current preschool and her family lived a few towns away. During their 2-hour visit, I had scarcely heard James walk, come downstairs or clear his throat. I remember wondering, "What could he be doing upstairs for so long and be so quiet?"

Usually, he was doing laundry, completing sales spreadsheets for his company, or some task to keep busy while we were involved elsewhere. As we walked Christy and her mom to the front door to say good-bye, I looked up the long straight staircase and saw James' legs emerging from our papasan chair positioned directly under our loft's skylight. He was very still and immersed in something that had his rapt attention. He said "good-bye" and "nice meeting you" to their family, and Lilly and I waved from the screened door until they drove away.

My curiosity had gotten the better of me, so although he was sitting in the chair just outside Marcus' doorway, I went up to investigate. Upon climbing the stairway, I saw him sitting with his legs crossed and a familiar cover between his open hands. It was a Bible. This looks like the Bible I bought him for our anniversary last Spring!

"Hi, you were so quiet while we were hanging out down there, I wasn't sure what you were up to."

"Yeah, I've just been reading," he said nondescriptly.

"Oh, that looks like the Bible I bought you last May for our anniversary. What did you decide to read?"

"I read the entire book of Matthew and now I am half-way through Mark," he replied calmly.

How can *he* be calm at a moment like this! I have been praying for so many years that he would read the Bible, fall in love with Jesus and give his life to HIM! This is the most awesome day of my life!

"Wow, that's so great. I would love to hear more! Marcus will be waking up soon, please let me know when and I'll come get him. I don't want to disturb your reading. The girls had a blast. Thanks for letting them come over today. Christy is a fun girl, and Lilly and she laugh up a storm. We'll be downstairs enjoying the sunshine until Marcus needs me."

"Jesus, this is like 1,000, no 2,000 answered prayers!" I celebrated, silently. "I cannot believe my ears! Did James say he read a book for 2 hours, and not only a book, but he's reading the BIBLE?"

James' famous quote since college has been, "I am illiterate except for reading the Sports Page." This is not only completely untrue, since James is a genius and reads content for work all the time, but the hundreds of books lining his bookshelves from before I met him were evidence to the contrary. He had lost his love of reading somewhere along life's path and the first book he picked up was the Bible. Awesome. This is the best day ever. I could barely wait until we put the kids to bed after dinner, and then I could really ask him what made him read this today, what he learned, and a thousand other questions. I would have to hide my elation and try to stay calm and just be a good listener. Too many questions will put him off and scare him away from sharing his deep thoughts with me, and I would seem pushy or bossy by peppering him with an inquisition. This is the best news I have had all year!

Dinner came and went, bathtime, bedtime stories and prayers, and then the sweet time when we both kissed the kids good-night in their own rooms. Afterwards, we had a few moments to talk downstairs on the couch.

My excitement was too high to recall the details of conversation from that

watershed evening. He felt drawn to picking it up and reading it that

afternoon. The Bible had been put away in a drawer for months, and he had

not given it much thought. (He was really quite annoyed when I had given it to

him which he tried to hide. Ten years later, he admitted in a testimony video

that he was angry I had wasted an anniversary gift on a Bible, thinking, "What

kind of *gift* is this?")

Over the past three years since I had been pregnant with Marcus, I

insisted on switching over all of our radio stations at home and in the car with

the children to Christian radio stations. Radio conversation had grown lewd,

perverse, and so over-the-top inappropriate for kids, I dreaded the thought of

Lilly being poisoned by these influences. We rode hours and hours each week

in one of our two cars, so in January 2004, while pregnant with Marcus, I made

the difficult switch from my favorite morning DJ's, who felt like family, to

strangers playing songs I had never heard and artists whose names were

obscure. I forced myself to remain tuned to those stations until they became

familiar. As a former rock-n-roll junkie and avid concertgoer, this was a hard

addiction to break. However, this was one of the absolute wisest decisions I have made for our family. (Now, I am a Christian worship music junkie and I am never going back.)

Once I began eating, sleeping and breathing all Chrstian music, videos, and magazines, I began hearing of rock concerts in our area. On K-Love, Moody, and FISH FM in Chicagoland, we began hearing about shows coming with artists I loved. I took James to see Petra on their farewell tour in 2005 the week before Marcus' choking incident. Now, there were artists coming to the House of Blues as well as a Christian music festival in the summer. I was praying he would say "Yes", when I invited him to go with me to both events.

Sure enough, we had the blessing to travel downtown Chicago for an exciting night to see some Godly and very relatable talents in Jeremy Camp and Toby Mac at the House of Blues. This is a venue James had visited numerous times throughout the years with high school and college friends or co-workers. I had never gone there, as once I hit 21, I was not in that scene much anymore. Most of my friends did not want to travel to the city, so I went to venues in the suburbs, occasionally. On this particular night, we heard the Gospel presented in a way by these two men in such a powerful way that James was clearly touched. His heart began to soften, and he said things to me on the ride home that I would not have expected to be spoken. A brand new beginning for our family was emerging and it was one of the most thoroughly exciting phenomena to witness unfold before my very eyes.

That summer, a few months later, the 12-hour "Ignite Chicago" stadium event was touting 10 bands and 10,000 fans in Schaumburg, Illinois. As James had begun listening to these songs on the radio with the kids in the car, he was familiar with several artist names, especially Casting Crowns and David Crowder Band. Next thing we knew, I was receiving 2 FREE K-Love tickets and backstage passes to meet Casting Crowns on the day of the event in July. They were only on the Christian music scene 3 short years after skyrocketing to stardom. They had numerous #1 hits and their humility of maintaining their Youth Ministry calling while still writing songs and touring the nation were extremely unique.

That Saturday in July 2007 was extraordinarily hot. We went prepared with a backpack of things to accompany us for the next 10-12 hours of standing down front near the stage pit, taking turns using the bathroom so as to not lose our spot. James had learned lots of techniques in his heavy metal and rock-n-roll days. I laughed at the strategies he knew and how to get the best vantage point at these events. We got there before the bands took the stage and planted ourselves for the duration of the event. Little did we know, this day would go down in history for us and our marriage. (This annual summer event became an incredible highlight for us in our family as we began taking the kids several years later.)

Half-way through the day, we had enjoyed a rapper K-52, Barlow Girl, some duos and a country artist and then the time had come to cash in on those backstage passes about 4 hours prior to Casting Crowns headlining the night. We wove our way through the massive hot crowd, up flights of concrete stairs at the outdoor baseball stadium until we found the main concourse.

Signs towards concessions and bathrooms bombarded us as we fought our way through 1,000's of people until we discovered the VIP elevator that would take us up to the top floor suite to meet Mark Hall and his band. Our lanyards were ready to pass us through security, up the elevator, and into the bright room full of sunlight streaming through the windowed-walls of the suite.

The minutes flew by as we shook hands with the band members, had them sign our laminated lanyard cards with their names and favorite Bible verses. All of this happened in a flash of time and in a blink, we were past them, the line was forming behind us, and we were standing reading the verses that each of them wrote. Mark Hall signed "Ps 1" with a picture of a crown in black sharpie. I did not know what Psalm 1 was about nor had I recalled ever paying attention to reading it, carefully. I knew that I would look it up when I got home! (Ironically, due to my daughter's 2nd grade teacher having the students memorize this Psalm, I have it also memorized and choose to recite it almost every morning before I leave the house over 15 years later. I encourage you to read it!) Melody, the violinist signed my lanyard with a smile and music notes, and her husband, Juan the guitarist, and Melanie, the vocalist and piano player, and so on. We were so blessed by this encounter, catching a small glimpse into the kindness of their hearts as they shook our hands, smiled, and signed our cards. (This is a far cry from my first concert and going backstage to meet Def Leppard in 1988! I reflected how there were no comparisons between these two memories, not even close!) James and I were beginning to understand a subculture in America we had never known existed, and what we almost completely missed out on, but the Lord above had grace and mercy to reveal Himself to me first, and then begin to mold and draw James and our kids, too. What an awesome and gracious God.

After coming back from the "meet and greet", we had to find a way back down to the front near the stage for the closing bands. Somehow, James was clever enough to find gaps in the crowd to weave his way hundreds of yards back up to the front in the steamy humidity of the night amongst the crowds of people. We found ourselves close enough to see beads of sweat pouring down the musicians' faces from under the hot stage lights. This was surely a night we would not forget!

As the night gained momentum, David Crowder Band took the stage and the sunset over the horizon was colorful and breathtaking from within the outdoor stadium. People were laughing and full of joy, engaging in pleasant conversation, and singing their faces off. We knew several of the songs from the radio and others we simply enjoyed and joined in on the repeated choruses. Soon, Casting Crowns took the stage. I sang along with my eyes closed, belting out the familiar lyrics to songs like, "Praise you in the Storm", "We are the Body" (my personal favorite that I had sung as a solo at our church one Sunday), and "Voice of Truth". As the verses and chorus crescendoed, I looked to my left at James in the darkness of the night, stage lights reflecting off his face, and saw a single tear roll down his right cheek. I broke. My husband was being touched by His Creator and he was feeling something he had never felt before. Later, he would tell me that was the moment when he gave himself to Jesus Christ, His Lord and Savior. That was James' moment of Truth. Awesome! This was the beginning of a completely revolutionized McKnight Family, in absolutely every possible way.

Chapter 27:   Heaven

Revelation 19:4 - "He will wipe away every tear from their eyes, there will be no more death, nor crying, nor sorrow and there shall be no more pain."

Throughout the night of January 19th into the wee hours of the 20th, 2023, I had been on this roller coaster journey of watching monitors flashing, and God intervening and doing miracles. My Mom spoke words of life about My God and Savior as I sang worship music and songs of praise over her. The Lord, Our Jehovah Rapha, did dozens of miracles that night. First, Ned left me alone with her as only one visitor was allowed. He is so incredibly devoted, that he had not left her side for 72 hours and was not about to go. The Lord moved in his heart to let me be the one to stay with her once I arrived from Chicago. This allowed me to bind the enemy, cast out the spirits of sickness and infirmity and death from her ICU room and ask the Lord and His Heavenly angelic Host to come and minister to her severely broken body. Next, my Mom and I had hours in which to talk, express our love, share our hearts, extend forgiveness, and experience a sanctuary of praise in that ICU. Solitude allowed our hearts to connect in a more profound way than ever before over 50 years. Not when I was in her womb, or as a toddler, had we been this close and intimate. We did not even experience this closeness as she imparted motherly wisdom to me after giving birth to my own children. This sacred night of prayer, worship, holding her hands, massaging her feet, applying lotion to her burning skin, putting cool washcloths on her forehead, and pressing wet sponges to her lips were some of the sweetest, most intimate moments I will cherish for eternity.

My Mom, the precocious child turned fiercely independent and outspoken woman, as well as highly accomplished, lay before me and allowed me to care for her, serve her, and lavish love on her. The hours that ensued once Ned and Corey arrived after 2:45 am are ones that are deeply personal to our family and I would be remiss in sharing details that truly only the three of us will personally ever know and relive. Even James, my beloved children, and Daisy's closest friends could never truly grasp the events of those farewell hours.

All night I contended for miracles. God was doing them, I was seeing them, and many were praying. I believed that she would live and not die and see the Goodness of the Lord in the land of the living (Psalm 27). As the hours rolled by, we saw some dire changes in her condition that left me resolved, yet wondering how God would ultimately respond to my prayers. Over thirty-three years, my heart's cry was that before her last breath, she would say "Yes!" to Jesus and be with Him for eternity. In this moment now, whether that would mean he resurrected her broken organs, restored all functioning, or brought her home to be with Him was yet to be seen. I longed for her to know she was treasured, loved and being healed by Him, and then given a place He intricately prepared just for her in Heaven that would exceed every expectation of beauty her mind could conceive. If she were to leave earth now, I had solace that she would be delivered from all pain, trauma and anguish.

All of us believed we would not say good-bye to her for at least 20 more years as her mother lived until 102-years-old, and longevity ran in the family. Almost everyone agreed Mom's energy level and zeal for life would take her near or past her own mother's years on earth. We were still feeling incredulous about the turn of events that transpired only 72-hours or so earlier. We were only acquainted with a vivacious and energetic woman who was always the center of all the action in any one place. This Daisy who could no longer speak or breathe properly on her own was one none of us recognized.

On that balmy Florida morning as the sun crested the horizon, just before sunrise, we pledged our love and spoke what had gone unspoken before our opportunity was stolen. My heart was bursting with pain after her last heartbeat sounded. We were in shock. We had few words and many tears as we all held hands and said all that was on our hearts to say. It was a sacred and tender moment filled with shock and grief beyond words. I was in disbelief for several minutes. All night, I believed the Lord would do a miracle, even bringing new organs or resurrecting the degrading ones, or resurrecting her even after her last breath.

My body finally caught up to the reality of being awake almost 30 hours yet all I cared about was my sweet mother. We drove silently home and each needed some time to be on our own to rest and process all we had just endured. Walking into the guest room of my parents' beloved house that was filled with a rich archive of memories, I was so distraught. This house without her would never again be as vibrant. They dreamed of retiring here for so long and their dream had become a welcomed reality. Their forty-year marriage had weathered hundreds of hardships and rejoiced on many mountaintops, too. These golden years had been full of the most joy either had experienced in eight decades on earth. I had prayed over thirty years for my Mom to surrender to Jesus and my soul was in anguish.

I cried out to the Lord, "Lord, I need to know where she is! I cannot sleep until I know."

"I have her," I heard immediately and without pause.

It was not a whisper, it was not a shout. It was crystal clear. With those words, I was able to lay my head down for a desperately short nap which my body urged me to take. Tears of mixed emotions cascaded onto the pillow as I closed my eyes and cried for joy at hearing His words. I know my Daddy's voice from Heaven when He speaks to me. He told me, "I have her". There is no greater place for anyone to be, than in the loving arms of Jesus. My Mom had chosen Him after almost eight decades on this earth with so many trials and triumphs, valleys and mountain top experiences. Now, she is dancing with Our Father God in His fields of Grace.

Epilogue

Saying "yes" to Jesus as your Lord and Savior and living for Him is the most important decision a person can ever make. Not only will He forgive your sins, exchange His perfect sinless life with your guilt-ridden one, but additionally, He will seal you with His Holy Spirit who preserves you for the day of redemption. He will indelibly record your name in the Lamb's Book of Life, and you will bask in Heaven for all eternity once your soul leaves earth. From the day you make this choice to surrender self-worship and choose instead to worship Jesus alone, the Holy Spirit comes to live inside you as His holy temple, and you begin ushering Heaven to come invade the earth. Jesus' Blood covers you, He protects you, and the Holy Spirit of God gives you wisdom, comfort, revelation of the Word of God (the Bible), and fellowship with God the Father, Jesus the Son and the God the Holy Spirit. You receive a new heart (Ezekiel 36) and a new mind (I Cor 2:16) and you become a brand new, one of a kind unique creation (II Cor 5:17). This is the most remarkable metamorphosis the earth has ever witnessed. I urge you to stop, pray, and be authentic in your prayer to ask Jesus to forgive you of your sins, to ask Him to be Lord and Savior over your life, and He will begin to fill you with inexplicable joy and peace that you have never known before. He is a Good

and Awesome God!

Acknowledgements

There are far too many people to thank by name at the many churches we have attended, friends and pastors who prayed our marriage from ashes to beauty, and have walked alongside us these many decades. I want to thank our parents, grandparents, family members and dear brothers and sisters in Christ who have guided us, prayed for us, held our arms up in the battle, and still pray for us. These men and women who do life with us both near and far are a priceless gift from the Lord Himself to allow us to keep standing on the Promises of God, reflecting on what He has done and believing for what He will do. (Remnant Rising crew, a shout out to all of you in Illinois! We would not know Holy Spirit like we do today without each one of you. You are all a gift to the Kingdom of Heaven.)

I cannot truly express the depth of thanksgiving I feel down to the bottom of my toes (because my heart is not deep enough!) to thank my covenant husband who could have tired of a nagging and flawed wife who tore him down with her words. You never gave up on me (us) even when I could have given up on myself. But God. Tim, you are loyal, faithful, dedicated, and a hard-working man of faith who perseveres through massive challenges and intense trials. I admire you for these qualities and more.

To our incredible children, Abigail and Lucas, you have been invaluable sanctifiers for me, revealing the gravity of my own sin and how it caused you great pain. I am grateful to the Lord for giving you to me as gifts to be your Mama and to be humbled by Him so I could recognize the error of my ways, turn from pride and ask you to forgive me. Thank you for choosing forgiveness when I did not deserve it and opening your hearts up to me. The gift of relationship we have now that you are adults is precious to me. You have taught me more than you will ever fully comprehend.

I have to thank my very closest sister on earth for leading me to a Bible study in 2005 which was the watershed moment in my life. Angie, you have cried with me, celebrated with me, laughed with me, and prayed with me more than anyone else on the planet. I cannot wait to spend the rest of eternity with you loving Jesus together. It has been a treasure beyond words.

I am grateful for God's Word, the Bible which is truly alive! (Heb 4:12- "It is living and active, sharper than a double-edged sword and II Tim 3:16 - All Scripture is breathed out by the Holy Spirit.) We pray His Word over our marriage, family, children, future son and daughter-in-law and grandchildren yet to be born. We believe III John 4 as a verse of declaration that says, "{We} have no greater joy than to know that our children are walking in the Truth." We believe that our legacy has been permanently changed by Jesus Christ and His Blood and all future generations will be walking in His fullness that He planned for each one of them by His abundant Grace.

My heartiest gratitude is for Our Lord and Savior, Jesus Christ. (Jesus, you are my BFF. Hands down.) He is the greatest Creator of all things, including miracles of resurrection and redemption. He brings dead hearts and dead marriages to life. Jesus led a perfect, sinless life on earth and gave Himself as a blood sacrifice on the cross as fully God and fully man in order to bridge the great divide between sinful man and a perfectly Holy Father God. Jesus as the perfect "Lamb of God" made salvation possible. Apart from His atoning sacrifice by willingly laying His life down for mankind, I would have no story to share, no hope, and no fresh outlook on living a Heavenly agenda on this earth. Lord, you made me new, sent Your Holy Spirit to come live in me, and did a radical makeover from the inside out. This has been a revolutionary roller coaster ride with you, and I have had the time of my life.

Finally, I am thankful for testimonies! God's works on earth become our testimonies (our personal stories) to witness to His magnificent power.

Testimonies are faith builders. What you are holding in your hands is a compilation of testimonies to what God can do with a broken, angry, wounded girl and transform her into a blood-bought daughter of the Living King Jesus. He removed my heart of stone and gave me a heart of flesh to begin living and loving the way He intended. I was insolent, self-centered and full of hate. He taught me forgiveness and freedom. He allowed me to believe that His love is intended for me and broke the walls of hostility that kept me from feeling lovable. He pursued me until I stopped, turned around, and said "yes" to all He wanted to purge from my heart, mind, soul and spirit. He took me from being pro-choice to pro-Life, from ignoring pain in others to caring for the least of these, from keeping an iron-tight grip on every penny I had and allowing me to give generously to God's Kingdom agenda on earth. (My husband has single handedly modeled more about generosity than any other human in my life.)

I am thankful for the New Life you gave me, Lord Jesus! It has been quite a journey!

THE BEST IS YET TO COME!

About the Author

Leann Landstrom, her husband Tim, of 25 years, their two amazing college-aged redheads, and their two gorgeous kittens live in the suburbs of Nashville, Tennessee where the Lord led them in 2023 by His still small voice. You will find them reading the Word, worshiping Him, taking bike rides and walks, drinking a strong cup of coffee and marveling at the Goodness of God. Apart from Him, they would not be together today enjoying the benefits of God's faithfulness to them as individuals or in their marriage. God is Good!

Leann has been a teacher and junior high ministry leader for 15 years and adores middle schoolers and children of all ages. She is an avid swimmer, cyclist, and loves being barefoot in the outdoors as often as possible. Tim has owned his own energy business at home for over 20 years which has allowed him to be a hands-on dad, sports coach to their children as well as others, and to spend hundreds of hours with brothers in Christ exploring the facets of Jesus in everyday life.

Feedback If you have questions about knowing Him, were impacted by our story, or have a comment, please reach out to me on Facebook: **Leann**

Landstrom and leave a private message! I will read it and respond as soon as I am able. Sending encouragement through words and prayer are some of our greatest privileges. God's abundant blessings on you as you seek and follow Jesus! You will not regret a moment. :)

Prayer

My family and I have been blessed to come to know the Lord at
different times, over many generations of prayerful warriors interceding on
our behalf. I know my Dad's Mother was a praying woman, my husband's own
mother and his great-grandmother and surely others in both of our lineages.
Prayer sparks supernatural things to happen and the Lord longs to answer
prayers of salvation for those you love. Begin praying scriptures for your lost
loved ones by inserting their names into verses that you pray back to the Lord.
He wrote His word, and this is His Love Language. Here are some verses I
have prayed for the last several decades:

"Lord, you say in your word that you want none to perish, and all to
come to repentance, so I ask you to save _____." (II Peter 3:9)

"Lord, you tell us in Your Word that you peeled the scales of Saul's
eyes before he became Paul and I ask you to peel the scale's off _____ eyes in
the Mighty and Matchless Name of Jesus." (Acts 9:18)

"Lord Jesus, you tell us in Your Word that you can take a heart of stone
and make it a heart of flesh. I am asking you to give _____ a heart of flesh. In
Jesus' Name. (Ezek 36:26)

"Lord, in John 6:44 you tell us that no one comes to the Father unless the Father draws them to Himself. I ask you to draw these people I love, _____, to Yourself. You are the only one who can save."

"Lord, in Ephesians 1:18, you tell us that you can enlighten the eyes of our hearts and _____ needs his/her heart enlightened to see and know you. I ask You to reveal Yourself to _____. In the powerful name of Jesus we pray. Amen."

"Lord, it says in your Word that you did not appoint us unto wrath, but unto Salvation (I Thess 5:9). You desire for _____ to be saved. You tell us this in Luke when Jesus said Himself, "I came to seek and save that which is lost (Luke 19:9-10).""

Acts 16:31 says, "Believe in the Lord Jesus, and you will be saved, you and your household." Lord, because you saved me, you desire to save my whole household, including, _____ .

Praying God's Word back to Him is extraordinarily powerful! Find verses that captivate you for the prayers and petitions of your heart and bring them to the Lord, praying people's names in those passages. You will draw closer to the Lord during your time of prayer, and I believe Hope will begin to rise up in you as you pray! He is a Mighty, Awesome and Powerful God who is also Our Perfect Father. He is infinitely good at protecting us (Psalm 91) and providing (Phil 4:19) for us. We are never at a lack with Him (Psalm 23:1). He is Our Good Shepherd (John 10 and Psalm 23) and He listens to our prayers. God's Word even promises us that Jesus Himself intercedes (prays) on our behalf, continually (Hebrews 7:25).

I pray that you are blessed as you pray and come to know Jesus in a rich and life-changing way!

Made in the USA
Columbia, SC
12 May 2025

57780031R00161